# Science Knowledge for Primary Teachers

# Science Knowledge for Primary Teachers

Understanding the Science in the QCA Scheme

Linda Gillard

 David Fulton Publishers

This edition reprinted 2008 by Routledge
2 Park Square, Milton Park, Abingdon, Oxon OX14 4RN
Simultaneously published in the USA and Canada by Routledge
270 Madison Avenue, New York, NY 10016

First published in Great Britain by David Fulton Publishers 2005
Transferred to digital printing

Note: The right of Linda Gillard to be identified as the author of this work has been asserted by her in accordance with the Copyright, Designs and Patents Act 1988.

*British Library Cataloguing in Publication Data*
A catalogue record for this book is available from the British Library.

ISBN 1–84312–188–3

Typeset by FiSH Books, London

# Contents

To Bethany, Alison and Aaron, for asking the questions

# Preface

My first memory of a science lesson was in year six at primary school. I was in a very large class (there were 48 of us) and the teacher used a large water-filled container and a sewing needle to demonstrate how a compass worked and how the needle responded to magnets. We were all amazed that the needle floated, never mind its miraculous ability to point north. It is this ability of science to fascinate and explain that makes it such an enjoyable subject to teach and to learn.

With the introduction of the National Curriculum and science finally having a core place in the primary school, many teachers found themselves ill prepared for the task. The last fifteen years have seen huge advances and success in the teaching of primary science and there is a lot of stimulating and creative teaching taking place. This book provides background science knowledge for those new trainees and teachers who have, or believe themselves to have, insufficient knowledge and understanding of aspects of the science curriculum. Developing this knowledge and understanding should enable them to follow up children's ideas and explore explanations rather than present science as a body of facts to be memorised.

This book does not attempt to tell you how to teach, but explains the scientific concepts that you need to understand in order to teach primary science. By understanding these concepts, you will be able to listen to the children's ideas and have the confidence to develop creative ways of teaching science. To help you with this, each chapter includes information about the common misconceptions held by children and adults. This is always a good test of our own understanding; we need to recognise how these ideas do not fit with the science model and how they can be challenged.

The book is linked to the topics in the Qualifications and Curriculum Authority (QCA) scheme of work, but readers not using or unfamiliar with this scheme should still be able to find background science to a topic they are preparing to teach. Within the book, concepts are linked to recognisable situations and it attempts to present the information in a readable format. I hope that as a busy trainee or teacher you can find the section you need by using the bullet-pointed introduction at the beginning of each chapter. This indicates the topics included and should enable you to quickly locate the section required. By also reading the misconception section you will develop your understanding, and there are review activities and questions for you to consolidate and extend your learning.

The first chapter introduces the reader to the importance of teaching and learning science, its difficulties and misconceptions. The support provided by the QCA scheme of work is considered and the role of scientific enquiry and developing cross-curricular links are highlighted.

Chapters 2 to 5 explore biological ideas; human and plant biology, the environment and variation. In Chapter 5 current developments in gene technology are presented because this is an area of much current media coverage. Teachers will be faced with questions about cloning and DNA manipulation and although not a primary science topic, it is one that is important and which can be controversial. We are better placed to help children understand these controversies if we understand the science involved.

Chapters 6 to 8 explore chemical ideas and some basic geology. Chapter 7 introduces kinetic theory. This is a core idea that provides a basis for understanding other topics within the book. It purposefully does not include the expected diagrams of particles in a solid, a liquid and a gas to encourage the reader to think about the ideas and relationships being presented.

Chapters 9 to 14 explore physics topics. Understanding forces is often problematical and two chapters have been included, separated into key stages one and two, but the reader is recommended to read both. Ideas taught in key stage two require an understanding of the ideas already presented in key stage one and those working in key stage one need to appreciate how the ideas will be developed. The relationship between night and day and the phases of the moon are included in the chapter on light. The last chapter on energy brings together some of the ideas already met in the book and shows how an understanding of energy and energy transfer can be applied.

A bibliography is included so that you can find further reading on teaching primary science and misconceptions in science. The National Curriculum is referenced by its authors, the DfEE and the QCA. The DfEE (Department for Education and Employment) has now been superseded by the DfES (Department for Education and Skills).

I would like to thank several people who have helped in the production of this book. My colleagues and the trainees at Roehampton University provided a forum for discussing science ideas and misconceptions. In particular, I would like to thank Virginia Whitby, who carried out research into the use of the QCA scheme and who has been very supportive and generously shared her findings. Finally, my husband Tom was the first reader of the book and has given invaluable feedback on the content and has even learnt something!

Linda Gillard
December 2004

# CHAPTER 1

# Exploring science ideas

## QCA Units

This chapter supports the teaching of the following QCA unit:

- Enquiry in environmental and technological contexts

## National Curriculum

This chapter supports the following sections of the National Curriculum:

- Key stage 1 Scientific enquiry, Breadth of study
- Key stage 2 Scientific enquiry, Breadth of study

By reading and reflecting on this chapter, you should have developed your learning about science as a core subject in the National Curriculum and be able to:

- Explain why it is important to develop your science knowledge and understanding.
- Explain why science is hard to learn.
- Recognise the role of the QCA scheme in supporting the teaching of science.
- Discuss the importance of teaching and learning about scientific enquiry.
- Develop links between science and other areas of the curriculum such as literacy, numeracy and ICT.

## The importance of learning science

Science is a core subject in the National Curriculum and a subject that excites and motivates pupils because it provides a way of making sense of the world in which they live. Young children naturally ask questions and good science teaching provides a framework for focusing questions and for actively seeking answers. The concern for many adults is that they do not know the answers and when children experiment and try things out they may get results that the adult is unable to explain. I hope that reading this book will increase your confidence in your science knowledge and understanding so that you are able to answer children's questions appropriately. In some instances, an appropriate answer might be, 'That's a very interesting question. What could we do to find out the answer?'

Many readers of this book will have learnt science during their secondary education and have retained a recall of science facts and formulae, but in a disjointed and incomplete way and perhaps with inaccurate understanding of the concepts. I hope that reading this book will help you to see the links between scientific areas, so that the knowledge that you already have will be more complete and coherent. I also hope that, having used this book, you feel confident and able to access more areas of science through your own further reading and research.

At the end of a course developing science knowledge and understanding, one PGCE student said, 'You look at the world differently and it's fascinating. I am beginning to see.' I hope that you will begin to feel the same way.

In its introduction the National Curriculum document (1999) states:

> Science stimulates and excites pupils' curiosity about phenomena and events in the world around them. It also satisfies this curiosity with knowledge. Because science links direct practical experience with ideas, it can engage learners at many levels. Scientific method is about developing and evaluating explanations through experimental evidence and modelling. This is a spur to critical and creative thought. Through science, pupils understand how major scientific ideas contribute to technological change – impacting on industry, business and medicine and improving quality of life. Pupils recognise the cultural significance of science and trace its worldwide development. They learn to question and discuss science-based issues that may affect their own lives, the direction of society and the future of the world.
>
> (p. 15)

## Why is science hard to learn?

An important reason for science being hard to learn is that science is counter-intuitive. We each of us develop a range of personal explanations of the way the world works. These are often in conflict with the scientific explanation and because they are our own ideas that we have developed during our lifetime they are not easily changed. Our ideas make sense and so the science ideas seem strange and unrealistic. The nature of these ideas or misconceptions and how to make teaching more effective has been the basis of extensive research. The children's Learning in Science Research group at Leeds

University worked in collaboration with Leeds City Council Department of Education and produced a range of materials and analysis of children's learning. An excellent overview of this work can be found in Driver *et al.* (1997) and in the associated resource file. A primary science focused research project was the Science Process and Concept Exploration Project (1991) based at Liverpool University and Kings College, London. This project provided the basis for the Nuffield Primary Science Scheme that contains clear and colourful illustrations of pupils' ideas about a range of science topics.

The ideas and explanations that we all develop about the way the world works without the input of formal science teaching are built up during our lifetime and are the result of a wide range of experiences and so are not likely to be easily changed. These experiences are not just practical but include information given to us by others through conversation, reading and a range of media. Children may have a view of the Earth and space developed from science fiction and fantasy television programmes. We know from experience that if we stop pushing the supermarket trolley, it stops moving, so it is very difficult to accept a science teacher telling us that all objects will continue to move until something stops them. Watching space fantasy programmes may make us believe that attacking an enemy spaceship results in loud explosions, but our science teacher may say that sound cannot travel through a vacuum. The co-operative ones among us may well memorise this science information and use it to reply to questions our science teacher asks, but we don't really believe it and continue to hold our own views on how the world works; after all, we do need to shop and keep pushing the trolley!

These non-scientific ideas are called misconceptions, and research has shown that many of these are common to children from different backgrounds and different countries. This means that when we start teaching a topic we can plan to address these common misconceptions and need to find out what other ideas children already have. By developing our own understanding of science and knowledge of what these alternative ideas or misconceptions are, we are in a better position to teach science. If we know the difference between where children already are and where we want to take them, we are in a better position to develop an appropriate pathway.

The constructivist view of science teaching views learning as an active process during which the learner develops or constructs their own understanding. The learner selects and integrates new experiences into already held ideas, facts and experiences. This means that when we come across something new, we try to fit it into the framework that we already hold. We can add completely new information and ideas, modify ones already held, reject the new experience as an anomaly or interpret it in a way that fits with what we already believe. A good example of this latter process was a student teacher who believed that sugar would not dissolve in cold water. From experience with cups of tea, she thought it dissolved in hot water, but experience of seeing sugar in the bottom of a cold cup of tea had convinced her that sugar could not dissolve in cold water. When given water and sugar to test out her ideas, she added a drop of water to a large quantity of sugar and was convinced that she had proved her point! Further work was needed in order to develop her knowledge and understanding of solubility. This ability of learners to select aspects of what is being taught and to use them to build their own personal understanding means that there can be a huge difference between what the teacher is teaching and what the learner is learning.

A teaching approach based on constructivist ideas involves finding out about the ideas already held and then presenting situations that enable these ideas to be challenged and modified if necessary. It is important that the degree of challenge is not too great or the new ideas are rejected. The skill of the teacher is in presenting the small steps which can be integrated and which enable the gradual development of the far more powerful explanations of the world around us that science provides.

There are many different techniques to explore children's thinking, and popular ways include using concept cartoons developed by Naylor and Keogh (1996), making posters, sorting and classifying activities, concept mapping and a range of investigative activities involving predicting, explaining and practical experiments.

The constructivist teaching approach developed by Driver (1988) involves an orientation stage in which the pupils' interest and attention is gained, the learning is given a purpose and the situation is given a context. This is followed by the elicitation stage, in which children's ideas are explored. The next stage is the restructuring stage, in which the pupils are presented with a wide range of strategies with which to try out new ideas. After this, pupils should be given an opportunity to apply these new ideas in different contexts and then review their learning. This is a chance to consolidate their learning and to think about how their ideas and explanations have changed.

## The QCA scheme of work

In 1998, the Qualifications and Curriculum Authority (QCA), in conjunction with the Standards and Effectiveness Unit of the Department for Education and Employment, published an exemplar scheme of work. In the *Science Teacher's Guide* (1998) it states:

> This optional exemplar scheme of work illustrates how the National Curriculum programme of study and attainment targets in science for Key Stages 1 and 2 can be translated into a practical plan. It shows how science might be taught to groups of children attaining at the levels broadly appropriate for their age.

This guide and the update published in 2000 explains that the scheme is optional and that individual schools could decide whether or not to use it as a basis for their planning of science teaching.

> The original scheme of work plus the additional revised units can be used as a basis for work in science if a school wishes. However, there is no compulsion to use them and schools may use as little or as much of the material as they find helpful.

A brief review of the history of science teaching in primary schools provides an explanation of why such a scheme was produced and why at that time. As long ago as the 1960s, leading academics in the field of science education, through professional bodies such as the Association of Science Education, were advocating the inclusion of science in the primary curriculum. At that time scientific progress was rapid. The space race provided a major focus and new science and technology were becoming more important in our everyday lives. It was suggested that society needed to understand these scientific and technological developments, understand the underlying science concepts and be able to prepare new scientists to ensure worldwide competitive success. That such science education should start in the primary school was based on the belief that the primary school is the place where children develop a wide variety of interests, and that science should involve this natural exploration and investigation.

Various curriculum projects were developed based on these pedagogic ideas. The first was the Nuffield Junior Science Project in 1964, and this was followed in 1967 by Science 5/13, produced by the Schools Council. Later work by the Schools Council produced Learning Through Science in 1979. Unfortunately, despite enormous financial support given to some of these projects, the development of primary science education and the hoped for curriculum reform did not happen. One of the reasons suggested for this by the Association of Science Education and HMI was a lack of science knowledge and understanding by primary teachers. The 1980s saw a renewed impetus to develop science education in primary schools and resulted in the development of science as a core subject within the National Curriculum in 1988.

Many primary teachers had to implement the National Curriculum with very little or no science understanding themselves and a consequent very high level of anxiety. The format of the National Curriculum document was difficult to interpret and there were many changes made to the National Curriculum in the first few years after its introduction. In 1995 Sir Ron Dearing undertook a review of the National Curriculum and schools were promised that there would be no further changes until 2000. The current document, published in 1999, is the result of this review. Meanwhile, primary teachers were still trying to teach science and needed support. Many were avoiding some topics, notably those involving forces and electricity. The QCA produced a range of support documents, including the science scheme of work in 1998.

The scheme was introduced to support science education in primary schools by promoting and enhancing the quality of primary science, to provide for consistency and progression and to enable government agencies to target advice to schools. Many schools started using the QCA science scheme to help them manage their science teaching. Some used it as the basis for their teaching, others as a benchmark against which they could measure their own science scheme of work. It still continues to be the basis on which many schools and primary teachers plan their science teaching.

The scheme divides the curriculum into units and allocates these units to school years. It therefore provides a framework for continuity. Continuity is related to teaching and planning sequences so that the learners are given a framework that supports their learning. Individual pupils' progress depends on his or her own learning. The scheme provides support for this within each unit. The units start with an orientation and elicitation activity and then suggest further activities that will challenge pupils' ideas and introduce new experiences. At the end of each unit is a consolidation and review activity. This sequencing of activities supports teachers who lack confidence in their own subject knowledge because it indicates an order in which ideas and concepts can be effectively developed. Further support is given in the 'points to note' which highlight common misunderstandings and misconceptions as well as health and safety issues. The scheme only provides a framework and individual teachers need to adapt it to suit their own pupils and the school science timetable. As teachers' confidence in their science teaching has developed, there is the opportunity for teachers to be more creative in their teaching and to use the scheme even more flexibly so that they can produce interesting and exciting science lessons, relevant to the pupils in their own class.

## Scientific enquiry

Scientific enquiry is at the core of good primary science teaching. Practical work in science ranges from developing skills such as learning how to use a thermometer correctly to whole investigations in which pupils design, carry out and interpret results in order to solve a problem. Other types of practical work provide opportunities to illustrate new ideas and observe carefully. Exploring flower structure by looking carefully at the individual parts and naming them, or dropping low air resistance balls of different masses and observing that they fall at the same rate, are good examples. Different types of practical work are suitable for different purposes, but whenever children are engaged in practical work in science it is important that they know what they are doing and what the purpose is. Most children enjoy the opportunity to be actively involved in lessons and enjoy practical work. However, it is possible for them to carry out this work, follow instructions carefully and work to achieve what they perceive to be the right answers without developing an understanding of the science skills or concepts involved. The pupils appear active and involved but they are not necessarily learning what was intended.

Science skills and the procedures used in carrying out a scientific enquiry need to be taught explicitly. Skills include learning to use a range of scientific instruments and being able to take measurements with the required degree of accuracy. So pupils need to learn to use a balance, a magnifying glass, a ruler and a thermometer and how to measure the volume of liquids. Importantly, they also need to learn which measurement to take and when, and how precise the measurement needs to be. This involves making decisions. So if we watch a dandelion seed fall to the ground and we want to know how long it takes, we could use a stopwatch and measure the time. Given that it takes us time to react to what we see and start and stop the watch, recording to the nearest second is probably as accurate as we can manage. Yet children will record to one hundredth of a second because this is what the stopwatch shows and because they think this is a more accurate result. In the same experiment, it would be important to always drop the seed from the same height. Knowing that the height needs to be measured is a different skill from being able to use a ruler. When using a ruler do we need to measure to the nearest metre or centimetre or millimetre? How many times do we need to take the measurements in order to feel confident in our results? What do we do about readings that do not fit into the general pattern? How to make these decisions needs to be taught.

The procedures of scientific enquiry as given in the National Curriculum include planning, obtaining and presenting evidence and considering evidence and evaluating. These procedures are to be developed through the context of the rest of the curriculum and based on the premise that ideas and evidence in science are the result of collecting evidence, asking questions, creative thinking and testing our ideas to find causal links. As with concepts, there needs to be progression in children's ideas about the procedures of science and this requires planning. The QCA scheme of work has integrated the development of experimental and investigative science into each unit and the development of the three strands – planning, obtaining evidence and considering evidence – is outlined clearly in the teacher's guide. Developing the skills and processes of science is such a huge topic that you are advised to read much further on this topic in the many science pedagogy books that are available, such as Harlen (2004), Hollins and Whitby (2001) and Sherrington (1998).

## Science and cross-curricular links

Science should not be an activity that takes place in isolation from the rest of the curriculum. If science were viewed as a body of facts and truths to be learned and memorised, then it would be possible to teach science in an objective way and carry out practical work to prove things. However, if science is perceived as a great exploration in which we endeavour to understand the world we live in, then we open up the possibility of thinking creatively about our world, entering into discussion and communicating and sharing our ideas with others and making science a social activity which links to other topics and which is relevant to our everyday lives.

The *Breadth of Study* section of the National Curriculum echoes this latter view. It states that the science knowledge, skills and understanding should be taught through familiar contexts and shows the links between science and many useful technological developments. It also suggests that different sorts of data and information should be used in science investigations. There is a need to use ICT-based sources and equipment effectively. This means learning to use ICT as a research tool, as well as to collect, present and analyse data. Developing the use of spreadsheets and databases allows pupils to collect, organise and interrogate data in a way that enables them to think about what the data means, rather than just how to present it in tables and lists. There are opportunities to develop and manipulate models of phenomena that are too small to see, such as molecules, or too big, such as planetary systems, to enable a much better understanding and greater engagement with the topic. Computer graphics that enable us to change our perspective and manipulate variables have enormous advantages if the process is engaged with in a meaningful way. Data loggers that collect and display experimental data have the advantage that the link between what is happening in an experimental situation and a graphical representation can be observed in real time. For example, using a data logger with temperature probes enables many measurements of the temperature of hot water in insulated and non-insulated containers to be taken and displayed as cooling curves. The focus for the children becomes the shape of the graphs and the reasons for the differences, rather than how to manage taking a sequence of temperature readings and recording them, then selecting a scale, plotting points and drawing the graph. These data-collection and presentation skills also need to be taught, but if they have already been mastered, then using ICT enables a focus on the interpretation of data and the science concepts involved.

Exploring science requires that we communicate our ideas in a variety of ways. This may involve discussing our initial ideas, researching other ideas and both planning and communicating our intentions with others. There are many natural links between science and literacy and it is important that these links are used. It can be motivating for children to plan an investigation in science from questions that arise from stories. Goldilocks and the three bears can be a starting point for looking at cooling, the three little pigs for exploring strength in structures, and the princess and the frog for finding out about life cycles. Science can be reported in a variety of ways. There is a formal way of reporting science and children will need to be introduced to the conventions of this type of writing, but they do not need to report all their science in this way. It can be more motivating and engaging to allow more imaginative reporting. After finding out about conditions needed for germination, how about reporting results in the form of an illustrated postcard from the seedlings describing the conditions they have been in? Results can be shown as a cartoon strip if there have been changes observed at given time intervals, or children can engage in imaginative writing in telling the story of what happens to an apple when we eat it or the life of a microbe trying to eke out a living on our teeth.

There are many links between science and mathematics. Science often involves taking measurements and recording them in tables and graphs, comparing measurements and sorting and classifying. Many scientific ideas can be summarised as mathematical formulae and so it is important to develop the links between these curriculum areas. Children can often forget to apply a skill developed and learnt in one curriculum area when they are working in a different context. It is important that we support this transfer of skills.

Science is an important part of the modern curriculum. It is relevant to all our lives. As teachers, we will educate both the future great scientists and those who will take their understanding of school science into their adult lives and use it as a background to their understanding of new scientific and technological developments as presented in the media. I hope that we will enable future generations to participate in informed debates about important issues such as cloning, electricity generation and the environmental effects of intensive fertiliser use and of growing genetically modified crops.

# CHAPTER 2

# Human biology

## QCA Units

This chapter supports the teaching of the following QCA units:

- Ourselves
- Health and growth
- Teeth and eating
- Moving and growing
- Keeping healthy
- Micro-organisms

## National Curriculum

This chapter supports the following sections of the National Curriculum:

- Key stage 1 Humans and other animals
- Key stage 2 Humans and other animals

By reading and reflecting on this chapter, you should have developed your learning about human biology and be able to:

- Understand and explain the role of bones, joints and muscles in the working of the human skeleton.
- Describe the structure and explain the function of the heart in the circulatory system and explain the long-term and short-term effects of exercise on pulse rate.

- Describe the role of different nutrients and explain the importance of having a balanced diet.
- Describe how different types of teeth are adapted for different functions and relate this to different diets and explain how tooth decay occurs.
- Recall that microbes are both beneficial and harmful and cite examples.

## The human skeleton: bones, joints and muscles

Try to imagine what you would look like if you did not have a skeleton. Imagine (or actually get hold of) some cotton wool and try to model a human shape. What is the difficulty? Can you get a better-shaped model human if you add a few cocktail sticks? How and where do you need to arrange these sticks? Thinking about this shows us that we need a supporting structure, and this is the skeleton's main function. The skeleton needs certain properties to be effective in supporting the rest of the body. It must be rigid and strong but not too heavy, and have the ability to repair itself if damaged and to get bigger as the whole body grows. The human skeleton is made up of bones and cartilage. The long bones in our limbs are good examples of bones that perform this structural function and which have these properties. They are able to grow and repair because they are made up of individual living cells embedded in a chemical matrix. This background material is a calcium compound for rigidity and strength, mixed with proteins for some flexibility so that bones are not brittle. Bones have a blood supply so that the substance of the bones can be removed and replaced and the cells kept alive. The centre of these long bones is not bone but contains bone marrow, which makes them lighter. In birds, the centre of the bones are hollow, which makes them very light – essential for flight.

## Joints

If you return mentally to your cotton wool and cocktail stick model, you may still be dissatisfied with it as a model because it is not very manoeuvrable and can easily fall apart. We need to hold the ends of the sticks together and may need to cut the sticks in half to enable the arms and legs to bend in the middle. In the same way, our bones need to be held together and we need **joints** to allow movement. Joints are held together by very strong, yet flexible and slightly **elastic**, material that makes up the **ligaments**. Imagine attaching two rods end to end with strong yet slightly stretchy string.

To enable the joint to function smoothly, the ends of the bones are covered with **cartilage**. This is soft, spongy and smooth so that, as the bones move, they do not grate against each other. Damage to the cartilage in our joints is very painful! As with any moving system, a lubricant is useful. In the case of a human joint, the space between the bone ends is filled with a lubricant called **synovial fluid**.

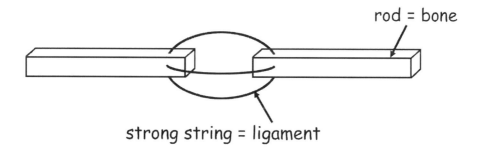

**Figure 2.1**  The model illustrating the role of ligaments

Some organs of the body are vitally important (we cannot survive if they are not working) and so need to be protected. Soft body tissues such as muscle and skin offer only limited protection. The skeleton also performs this protective function. Flat bones protect the brain by fully enclosing it. The heart and lungs are enclosed in a cage of bones, the ribs, and are further protected from the back by large flat shoulder blades. Making new blood cells is a third function of the skeleton. The spaces inside the long bones of the body are not left empty but are filled with bone marrow where new blood cells are made. This is a good example of utilising the available space in the body.

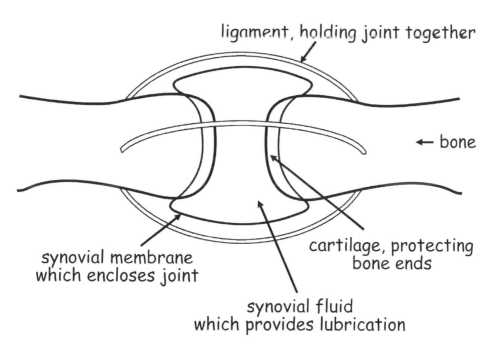

**Figure 2.2**  A simplified joint

## Muscles

The skeleton can only move if there are muscles attached to it. Muscles act by contracting. They are attached to the bones by very strong **tendons**. Tendons do not stretch and so if the muscle contracts, movement will happen. In the arm, the biceps muscle is attached by tendons to the shoulder blade, which is fixed in place, and to the lower arm bone, which is movable. When the muscle contracts, it pulls on the two tendons. The tendon attached to the shoulder blade provides firm anchorage, and the tendon attached to the lower arm transmits the pull of the contracting muscle, causing the lower arm to move upwards. At the same time, the elbow bends. In order to get the arm back to its original position, another muscle is needed because muscles work by contracting. The other muscle in the upper arm, the triceps, contracts and again the tendon attached to the shoulder blade cannot pull the shoulder down, but the end attached to the lower arm can cause it to move and it returns to its original position. Muscles can be stretched as they relax but only have power by contracting. All muscles act in opposing pairs: one of the pair contracts to cause one type of movement, and a second is needed to contract to cause the opposite movement.

## The heart and circulatory system

The human body is complex and made up of many different organs and tissues. Each individual cell in the body needs to be able to receive fresh supplies of oxygen and food molecules for **respiration**. The cells also need to be able to get rid of any waste chemicals that are made during their metabolism. **Metabolism** is the chemical activity that takes place in cells and enables both the cell and the whole body to function and live. Transporting substances around the body is the job of the blood. The blood picks up the oxygen as it flows through the lungs. Digested food gets into the blood through the wall of the small intestine. Waste carbon dioxide is picked up from the cells and escapes from the blood in the lungs, from where it is breathed out. To enable the blood to do all this fetching and carrying effectively, it flows in an organised way through the blood vessels that make up the circulatory system. Imagine a series of pipes all joined together. To get water to flow through them, you would need it all to flow in the same direction and something to push it along. The same is true of the circulatory system; the pipes are the blood vessels, the heart is the pump that pushes the blood along, and a system of valves ensures that the flow is in one direction.

Collecting oxygen and getting rid of carbon dioxide are such important jobs that there is a special branch of the circulatory system that ensures that all the blood is carried through the blood vessels in the lungs. This is called the pulmonary circulation. Blood is pumped from the right side of the heart the relatively short distance to the lungs. Blood rich in oxygen then flows back to the left side of the heart. From here it is pumped into blood vessels that carry the blood to the rest of the body. Much greater pressure is needed to pump blood to all areas of the body than is needed to pump blood just to the lungs. For this reason, the left side of the heart is bigger and has more muscle in its walls.

The heart acts like a double pump. One side (the right) is a smaller pump pushing blood to the lungs, and the other (the left) is larger and pushes blood around the body. In order to complete the circle, the blood returning from the lungs must enter the left side and be pumped round the body, and blood returning from the body must go to the right side, ready to be pumped to the lungs.

## Blood vessels

There are three different types of blood vessels. **Arteries** have a pulse and are found relatively deep in the body (except at pulse points). These vessels are muscular and elastic so that they are stretched as blood flows into them each time the heart pumps (or beats). They then spring back behind the surge of blood and so maintain the pressure and flow.

The main arteries branch to form smaller and narrower vessels. As they become smaller, they have thinner walls. Eventually, very small vessels called **capillaries** are formed. These very tiny vessels are in close contact with the cells of the body and have very thin and leaky walls. Some of the blood fluid (**plasma**) escapes from the blood system and surrounds and bathes the cells. In this fluid (now called **tissue fluid**) is the food and oxygen that the cells need. If your blood pressure is very high, then more fluid escapes and can build up and cause, for example, swollen ankles. Usually, most of this fluid drains back into the capillaries and these join up to make larger vessels called **veins**. Small veins join to make larger veins and carry the blood back to the heart.

The heart generates pressure that pushes the blood through the blood vessels, but as blood flows through the blood system, it loses some of this pressure. This is because it flows through a huge network of vessels and because the system leaks. In order to help maintain the flow and keep the blood going in one direction, there are valves. Large valves in the heart prevent the blood simply entering the heart and being pushed back the way it came in. More valves are found in the veins, as this is where the pressure is lowest.

## The effect of exercise

The heart is therefore at the centre of the circulatory system. Without the heart, the blood would not flow and the cells would stop functioning. When there is a greater demand on the cell, then the heart needs to work harder. There would be more demand if the body were more active. For example, if the brain cells are busy, they need more food and oxygen to provide the energy for nerve cell activity. Similarly, when the muscles are being used more during exercise, more food and oxygen needs to be delivered. The heart responds to these increased demands by beating harder and faster. After vigorous exercise we can feel our heart thumping in our chest. At other times, we

## a) Heart valves: 'parachute' valves

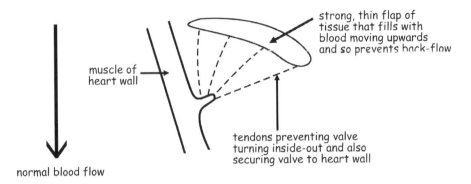

- strong, thin flap of tissue that fills with blood moving upwards and so prevents back-flow
- muscle of heart wall
- tendons preventing valve turning inside-out and also securing valve to heart wall
- normal blood flow

## b) Vein valves: 'pocket' valves

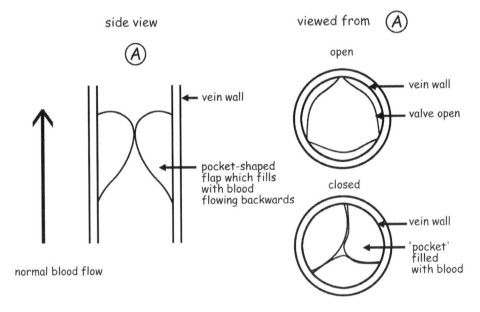

side view

(A)

- vein wall
- pocket-shaped flap which fills with blood flowing backwards

normal blood flow

viewed from (A)

open

- vein wall
- valve open

closed

- vein wall
- 'pocket' filled with blood

**Figure 2.3**  Valves in the circulatory system

can detect smaller variations by monitoring our pulse. The **pulse** is the surge of blood flowing in the artery each time the heart beats, so a change in pulse reflects a change to the heartbeat. The muscles of the body are working harder to enable us to stand up rather than sit down. Try taking your own pulse for 30 seconds while sitting resting. Then stand up for a couple of minutes and see if there is any difference. Jump up and down for a couple of minutes and try again!

As well as short-term changes to the heartbeat, there are longer-term changes. If we exercise and raise our heartbeat, then the muscle of the heart is also exercised and gets better at pumping. Athletes have lower pulse rates because their heart pumps more efficiently each time it beats. Exercise also improves the muscles that move the ribs and so our breathing is also more efficient, which means we are able to take in more oxygen with each breath. Blood, as it passes through the lungs, is better loaded with oxygen and so better at delivering it to the cells. Lack of exercise means the heart is less efficient and our breathing less effective. Our blood pressure increases and our breathing gets slightly faster to compensate, and so we get out of breath and tired more easily when we start exercising.

## Food, healthy eating and growth

All cells need food in order to function. The blood delivers this digested food to them, but how does the digested food get to the blood? And what sort of food do we need? All living things, including humans, need food and water in order to live. Food can be classified in many different ways: tasty or not tasty; fast or traditional; fruit or vegetables, etc., and all classifications can be useful. Biologists classify food into categories called **nutrients**. Nutrients are the chemicals that our body needs in the right amount and correct balance to keep us healthy. These nutrients are carbohydrates, fats, proteins, vitamins and minerals. We also need water, and to keep our digestive system working well we need to include fibre in our diet. Fibre is not a true nutrient because we do not digest it, but it passes through our system, working as a very effective scrubbing brush and it provides the bulk against which the muscles of the gut can push.

## Food and energy

The amount of food needed varies between individuals. It depends on their size, sex, age, lifestyle and activity level. Food provides our bodies with energy. We all need different amounts of energy and different foods provide different quantities of energy. Energy is measured in **joules** and **kilojoules**. By reading the ingredient lists on food packaging, we can find a value for the energy content, usually as energy content per 100 grams, so that comparisons between different foods are possible. Older readers will be familiar with energy being measured in calories, but this is an English rather than international measure, and so it is important to use kilojoules when working with children. Some foods are 'high energy' foods because they contain more energy per gram than others. Fats contain the most energy per gram, but carbohydrates, particularly sugars, provide us with an immediate energy boost. Sugars are quickly digested and absorbed into the blood and so can be quickly transported to the body cells for use in respiration. Too much sugar in the blood is not healthy, and so the body has mechanisms to remove it and store the excess in the muscles and liver (as glycogen) from where it can be quickly obtained if the blood sugar level drops. More complex carbohydrates, such as starches, take longer to digest but eventually are absorbed as sugars and used in the same way. Fats also take some time to digest and, once absorbed into the body, may be used to make important molecules, which can have either a structural role, such as in cell membranes, or a metabolic role, such as some hormones. Any excess fat in our diet is stored as a long-term energy reserve, capable of being converted to carbohydrates if they are not available. Proteins also contain energy but are more useful to the body to make structural components, such as muscles, and so once incorporated into the body will only be broken down if no other energy store is available. Proteins need to be eaten daily, as we do not store these bodybuilding components. The liver breaks down excess proteins in our diet and, as a result, produces a waste product called urea (which is filtered from the blood by the kidneys and leaves the body in the urine) and some carbohydrate.

The three main food groups provide us with energy. It is important to have sufficient energy for our needs or we become lethargic, and if we run out of stored energy food, we will suffer starvation. Too high a kilojoule intake will mean that the body will store the excess as fat, and we put on weight and may become obese. The key is balance between energy intake and energy expenditure and between the food types. Children need a different diet from adults as they are still growing, and growth requires energy and a different balance of the food groups.

## Food and health

All food groups contribute to our health and body maintenance. Proteins are the most important bodybuilding group and provide the structural molecules in all our tissues. Growth is making new tissues, either to increase in size or to replace damaged or worn-out tissues. Although proteins are the most important food group for growth, our bodies also need fats and carbohydrates as part of their structure and to function properly. It is important to have the right balance of food groups in our diet so that all are available as needed. Small amounts of vitamins and minerals are needed for the body to remain healthy. These are used in different ways: calcium and phosphorus make up the structure of bones and teeth, iron occurs in red blood cells and vitamins are involved in important chemical reactions such as those of respiration.

An unbalanced diet is also unhealthy and can lead to deficiency diseases, such as scurvy or rickets. It is possible to have sufficient energy in the diet and so not starve, but yet suffer from malnutrition – a lack of a dietary component. Our dietary needs vary during life. Our growth rate changes, as does our activity level and the demands made on the body. A menstruating woman needs more iron to renew her red blood cells, a pregnant or breastfeeding woman needs more calcium to meet the bone-development needs of her child, while an athlete in training has huge energy demands. There are no bad foods, only bad diets!

## Teeth

In order to gain the energy and structural building blocks from the food we eat, we need to digest it and absorb the small basic components into our blood and then distribute them to the rest of the body. The first stage of this process occurs in the mouth. Whether food is cooked or raw, either it is cut up into small pieces or we use our teeth to take bite-sized lumps from it. In our mouth the food is chewed and mixed with saliva. This initiates the process of digestion, and if we chew our food properly and don't gulp it down, we allow this to take place more effectively.

The teeth begin the process of making the food more accessible by chopping it up into smaller pieces. There are different types of teeth: at the front of the mouth are the incisors, next are the canines and at the back are the 'cheek' teeth, the premolars and molars. Each tooth type has a different function and so has a slightly different shape to make it effective. The incisors are for cutting and so have a flat front and shaped back (like a chisel), which gives them the ability to penetrate into food and take bite-sized pieces. Think about how you use your teeth when you bite into an apple, for example – look at the initial teeth marks that you make. The canines in humans are not so well developed as in dogs, which is where the name comes from. Canine teeth are pointed and allow food to be pierced. In wild animals the backward-pointing nature of these teeth means that they pierce and grip or rip prey and kill it.

The cheek teeth are squarer and their rough surfaces make them very good for chewing and crushing food. Once we have taken a bite, we use our tongue to manoeuvre the food between the cheek teeth, chew it to crush it and mix it with saliva so that it is easier to swallow. The cheek teeth nearest the front of the mouth are the premolars, and the ones at the back are the bigger but similar molars. Children do not have all their molars, and these back teeth develop after the first set of teeth, the milk teeth, have been replaced in late childhood.

## Teeth and diet

Different animals have teeth adapted for their diet. Carnivores, such as dogs and cats, have premolars and molars that are more triangular and act like scissors, cutting the meat up before swallowing. The food is not chewed because meat is mainly protein, and as saliva acts on carbohydrates, chewing and mixing the food with saliva would not have any effect. Herbivores have various adaptations. Sheep have well-developed upper incisors to cut grass, but they cut against a hard area of gum, not against lower incisors. This enables sheep to cut grass close to the ground. Vegetation causes more wear and tear on the teeth than meat, and so many herbivores have teeth that continue to grow throughout their lifetime. They also become more deeply ridged as some enamel is worn away, exposing the underlying layer of dentine, which then wears away more quickly. It is also noticeable that animals chew in different ways. Herbivores, such as camels, sheep and cows, move their jaws from side to side, so that the food is ground up between the top and bottom cheek teeth, whereas carnivores move their jaws up and down so that the food is cut up, using the cheek teeth like a pair of scissors.

All teeth have the same basic structure. They are made up of the part that shows above the gum and the root that anchors the tooth to the jawbone. Molars have more complex roots because they are bigger teeth. Teeth have a central cavity, which contains blood vessels, and a nerve, so the cells of the teeth are alive and sensitive.

## Tooth decay

Tooth decay results from our highly processed and sugar-laden diet. After eating, a microscopic layer of food remains as a coating on our teeth. This provides food for the many bacteria that are naturally found in our mouths. The bacterial activity produces acid which mixes with the bacteria and food layer on the teeth, forming **plaque**. The acid begins to react with the enamel and wear it away. The saliva we produce acts to neutralise the acid and as the food is used up, the bacterial activity slows. Cleaning our teeth both removes the plaque and neutralises the acid. To reduce tooth decay, we need to keep our teeth clean and not allow plaque to build up. It can become a hardened layer of scale, which is difficult to remove. We can reduce the frequency of acid build-up, for example, by not nibbling sweet foods all through the day, and we can strengthen our teeth by including fluoride in our diet. Fluoride is often added to water supplies for this purpose.

## Micro-organisms and health

**Micro-organisms** or **microbes** are very small organisms that can only be observed individually using a microscope. However, some make colonies that we can see easily with our eyes. The main types of microbes are bacteria, viruses and fungi. All of these groups of microbes contain species that are harmful and others that are helpful. Some micro-organisms cause disease (such as colds, flu, chickenpox) and others bring about decay, as seen when food rots or becomes mouldy and inedible. However, the decay process is very important in nature, or dead plants and animals would remain forever and the minerals that their bodies contain would not get recycled and would not be available for future generations. Microbes are also the basis of some important industries, including brewing, baking and, more recently, the production of medicines such as antibiotics and hormones.

Not all illnesses are caused by microbes. Some may be inherited conditions or caused by other factors, such as smoking, but infectious diseases are the result of microbes invading the body and being able to multiply. As living organisms, microbes will reproduce if they have the right conditions. For bacteria, this means a food supply, moisture and warmth, all of which our body supplies! The body has various defence mechanisms to prevent entry and also ways of attacking invaders, but sometimes we become ill as a result of infection. Outer defence is provided by the skin, which quickly seals and heals itself if broken. Body openings are protected – the nose has hairs and produces sticky mucus to capture invaders; the mouth leads to the digestive system and the stomach produces very strong acids that kill most bacteria entering with our food. When we eat badly infected food (that already has a flourishing colony of bacteria), we may suffer food poisoning, which results in the body getting rid of the infected food as quickly as it is able, giving us the well-recognised symptoms of sickness and diarrhoea! If we do become ill, our body has an immune system with special blood cells that work to overcome the bacteria and remove them from the body. The immune system is then prepared and able to recognise any further invasions from a similar organism. In this way, we build up our immunity to common illnesses during our lifetime. Unfortunately, some microbes are able to change and present a different appearance and so are not recognised. Consequently, we keep becoming ill with variations of the same illness. Colds and flu are good examples of this.

Diseases caused by bacteria, such as diphtheria and tetanus, can be prevented by **immunisation**. A small quantity of the dead or inactive bacteria is injected and this causes the immune system to react. If the real disease-causing organism then invades, it will be immediately recognised and the response will be quick enough to prevent the disease. **Antibiotics** are chemicals that kill bacteria and so are used to treat diseases caused by bacteria. Unfortunately, bacteria can also evolve and adapt to become resistant to antibiotics. This causes problems for hospitals when patients become infected with antibiotic-resistant strains; for example, tuberculosis (TB) now requires long treatment with multiple antibiotics because of resistant strains. There are vaccinations for some diseases caused by viruses, such as measles, polio and mumps, but some viral diseases can be more difficult to treat. In order to multiply, the virus takes over body cells and can remain hidden inside the cell during its development. It is only vulnerable to the attack of our immune system when the host cell is broken open and the virus is exposed before it is able to invade more cells. Some viruses can remain dormant in cells for long periods of time, giving no apparent disease symptoms. An example is the chickenpox virus that can remain in nerve cells, sometimes emerging to cause shingles many years after the original childhood illness.

Fungi and bacteria are closely associated with decay. We see mushrooms, toadstools and mould on things that are rotting and on food we have left lying around too long. We make use of this process to make garden compost. Fungi provide us with food such as edible mushrooms and the veins in blue cheese. Bacteria are used to make cheese and yoghurt from milk. Yeast is a fungus and is used in making bread, beer and wine.

## Common misconceptions

Children recognise that there are hard bones in the body and initially think of them all looking the same, like a dog bone in cartoons. There are many different shapes and sizes of bones in the body. Bones are not dead and their ability to grow and mend after breaking is evidence.

A simple view is of joints as being where bones meet and nothing holds them together. The role of joints in providing for movement and flexibility, rather than bones bending, needs to be added to a simple model of the skeleton. The different roles of cartilage, ligaments and tendons in joints are often confused. The misunderstanding that muscles can push as well as pull is overcome by understanding that muscles have to act in pairs.

Commonly, the heart is perceived as a valentine-shaped single pump and its dual role in pumping blood to the lungs and to the body is not fully understood. The role of the heart as a dual pump in generating different pressures to the pulmonary and body circulations is not appreciated. The large pressures needed to push blood to the body extremities would damage delicate lung tissue. The role of the blood in carrying gases in solution to the body cells is not understood. It is often thought that the lungs deliver oxygen to the body or at least to the heart and that the digestive system delivers food to the body. It needs to be clear that the blood system provides the network through which dissolved substances are transported.

Once food has disappeared from view it is thought to be inside the body. The nature of the digestive system as a tube passing through the body needs to be clear for the purpose of digestion to be apparent. Food entering a tunnel inside the body still needs to pass through the wall and get into the blood to be of any use. To do this, food needs to be broken down into its microscopic constituents. Diet is about eating, not about losing weight. Healthy eating is about balance: balance between different nutrients and balance between energy intake and energy use. All individuals are different and so, although it is possible to generalise about including fruit and vegetables in a healthy diet, quantities and proportions of carbohydrates, fats and proteins depend on age, sex and lifestyle.

Microbes are thought of as harmful and their beneficial effects are often overlooked. Decay is commonly associated with food spoilage and not with decomposition. Bacteria and viruses are not distinguished and so viruses are thought to respond to antibiotics.

## Review Questions

1  What are the three functions of the human skeleton?

2  What properties do bones need to have?

3  List four substances transported by the blood.

4  Where in the circulatory system are valves found, and what do they do?

5  Describe a balanced diet and explain the function of each of the nutrients.

6  What vitamins are commonly added to margarine and why are they added? What does the body use them for? What other staple foods have vitamins or minerals added to them?

7  Name some common diseases caused by bacteria and by viruses.

8  List some ways in which humans use microbes.

## Review Activities

1  Research what happens to bones when someone is suffering from arthritis.

2  Bend your fingers, flex your wrist, bend your elbow and move your arm at the shoulder. Identify the different types of movement possible. Can you find other examples of these types of movement elsewhere in your body?

3  Find out why some people need to have a pacemaker fitted or a bypass operation.

4  Research elephant's teeth and think about how they are adapted to the elephant's diet and longevity.

5  Find out more about the role of microbes in making cheese, yoghurt, bread, wine and beer.

# CHAPTER 3

# Plant biology

## QCA Units

This chapter supports the teaching of the following QCA units:

- Growing plants
- Helping plants to grow
- Life cycles

## National Curriculum

This chapter supports the following sections of the National Curriculum:

- Key stage 1 Life processes and green plants
- Key stage 2 Life processes and green plants

By reading and reflecting on this chapter, you should have developed your learning about plant biology and be able to:

- Explain why plants are living organisms and discuss similarities and differences in life processes between plants and animals.
- Describe the structure of a typical plant and be aware of the vast range of types.
- Explain the importance of sexual reproduction and describe the structure and function of plant sex organs.
- Illustrate and explain a flowering plant life cycle, distinguishing between pollination, fertilisation and seed dispersal, and between growth and germination.

●  Explain the importance of light, warmth and carbon dioxide to plants and relate healthy growth in plants to their need for water and minerals.

## Plants as living things

Living things are distinguished from non-living things because they carry out all of the characteristic life processes. These processes are often remembered by means of a mnemonic such as MRS GREN (Movement, Respiration, Sensitivity, Growth, Reproduction, Excretion, Nutrition). If able to observe a whole object or whole organism for some time then the decision about whether something is living or not is relatively easy. However, some of these life processes, such as respiration, occur all the time and others, such as reproduction, much less frequently. If only part of an organism or a particular stage in its **life cycle**, such as a seed, is presented, then it is difficult to make a decision without background knowledge of the whole organism and an understanding that what is being presented represents the whole organism. Children can become very confused if asked if a flower in a vase is living or not, but more easily understand that a whole plant is living. Plants also tend to exist over a much longer timescale than young children's attention span. Life cycles, such as those of trees, which may only be completed over hundreds of years, and movements that are too slow to capture in real time, need to be made accessible. The great age and size of some plants is truly awesome and the range of form and colour fascinating, but children need to have these brought to their attention, using real specimens, time-lapse photography and by providing opportunities for them to grow and nurture plants successfully.

## Movement

**Movement** is obvious in humans and most familiar animals because we both move from place to place and often move parts of our bodies even when stationary. Plants do not move from place to place except by growing. Time-lapse photography has been used to show how brambles creep across a woodland floor to occupy patches of sunlight, and how parasitic plants such as dodder have shoot tips that move in circles to increase the chance of them contacting a host plant stem. The tendrils of climbing plants act in a similar way. Other observable movements are the opening and closing of flowers, such as daisies, which close up at night. An interesting movement to observe is the way sunflower heads follow the sun during the day, which explains why they all face the same way when growing together in a field. There are a few instances of rapid movement by plants (for example, mimosa leaves fold up when touched), but all plants carry out small movements in turning their leaves to face the sun, opening flowers and bending towards the light.

## Respiration

**Respiration** is the process by which all living organisms release energy from their food so that they can carry out all their other functions and remain alive. This process takes place in every cell and needs both food and a supply of oxygen. In humans and other mammals, the oxygen is taken into the lungs and then into the blood system for delivery to the body cells during breathing. Breathing does not take place in plants, nor in many other animals, such as earthworms and insects, but respiration does. Oxygen gets into plants through tiny holes – called stomata – in the leaves and lenticels in stems. Plant roots get their oxygen from the air pockets in the soil and this is one reason why digging and aerating the soil is important for plants to grow well. During the daytime, leaves contain plenty of oxygen because the cells are making it as a by-product of photosynthesis (see below for details), but stems and roots always need to get their own supply from the air. All living things carry out respiration and most use oxygen, as this is the most efficient way to release energy from food. Some organisms can survive without oxygen by carrying out **anaerobic respiration**. When waterlogged, plant roots use anaerobic respiration and this results in alcohol being produced, but in very small quantities. Yeast also respires anaerobically and some varieties produce large quantities of alcohol – these varieties are used in brewing and wine making.

## Sensitivity

**Sensitivity** is the process by which organisms are aware of their environments, both external and internal. As humans, we sense what is going on around us using our sense organs – the eyes, ears, nose, mouth and skin, which give us our senses of sight, hearing, smell, taste and touch. We are also aware of our own bodies and get a range of information from internal sensors. This includes information about hunger, thirst, temperature, the state of the bowel and bladder, and positional information so that we are able to stand, sit and move. Other organisms are able to sense different things in the environment – for example, dolphins can detect and use high frequency sounds; some insects are sensitive to ultra-violet light, making what are plain white flowers to us look patterned to them; some bird species are sensitive to magnetic fields, which is an aid in migration, while dogs have an enhanced sensitivity to smells. Plants are sensitive to light and shoots grow towards the light. Roots are sensitive to both water and **gravity**, so plant roots will always grow downwards even when you plant the seed the wrong way up. Roots also grow towards wet areas, so will grow sideways if the water source is not deeper in the soil.

## Growth

**Growth** is making new organic material. This can lead to an increase in size, which is best measured as an increase in **biomass** or the mass of organic matter. This involves finding the mass of an organism without water. This means heating the organism until all the water has evaporated, by which time it is dead! This method is therefore not desirable and a simpler, but less accurate, wet mass can be used in schools. In plants, the amount of water can vary, but using well-watered plants is the best option. Water is continually being taken up by the roots and lost from the leaves during a process called **transpiration** and so if wet mass is to be used, the plants must have a plentiful supply of water to enable fairer comparisons to be made. It would obviously be unfair to compare a wilted with a non-wilted plant, or a plant in dry compost with one in wet compost.

Humans and other animals make new cells in various regions of their bodies. New bone cells are made to repair damage when a bone breaks and during childhood as bones grow to full size. We also continually grow new skin cells and lose them to create most household dust, as well as replace blood cells and repair torn muscles and other damaged tissues. Plants also repair themselves and we can observe the 'scar' tissue formed. However, plants only grow in length from the shoot and root tips. In deciduous trees, the growth regions overwinter as buds and these develop as more water is taken up in the spring. Trees and shrubs are also able to develop thicker woody stems, as there is a region just under the surface of the stem able to produce new cells. This new wood is produced at different rates during the year. In spring and summer, the growth rate is high and larger cells are produced, giving the wood a lighter appearance. In the autumn and winter, growth is much slower and denser wood is produced. Cutting across a tree trunk shows this alternating growth pattern and, as one light and one dark area takes a year to develop, we call this pattern annual rings, and counting them allows us to tell the age of the tree.

## Reproduction

Reproduction will be considered in more detail later in this chapter.

## Excretion

**Excretion** is the process by which organisms get rid of waste material that has been produced by the organism's metabolism. This means that faeces, which consist of undigested food, are not excreted but are passed from the body by **egestion**. However, urine is excreted because it has been made by breaking down proteins. This breakdown is also an example of metabolism, the chemical reactions that take place inside living cells. Plants make their own food and so do not have excess food to be got rid of, so plants do not produce urine. They do produce some unwanted chemicals and these are either deposited in the central dead wood of tree trunks, where they do no harm to the tree, or some are left in the leaves that drop off in autumn. All plants produce waste gases, both carbon dioxide from respiration and excess oxygen from **photosynthesis** in the green parts of the plant during the day. These diffuse out through the air spaces in the leaves and stems and then exit through the stomata and lenticels.

## Nutrition

**Nutrition** in mammals was discussed in Chapter 2 and plant nutrition, which involves photosynthesis, is discussed in more detail later in this chapter.

### Plant structure

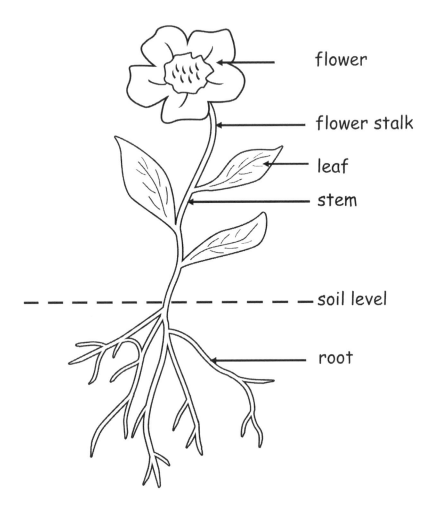

**Figure 3.1**   Plant structure

A typical flowering plant has a basic structure made up of a stem, leaves, roots and flowers. The stem spaces the leaves out so that they can trap sunlight. By looking at a plant from above, you can see that the leaves do not overlap, or in the case of a tree, look up through the canopy and see how very effectively the leaves are spaced out. The stem also contains the plant's water and food transport systems. Special cells (xylem) carry water from the roots to the leaves and other cells (phloem) carry the food made in the leaves to other areas of the plant, where it is needed for growth and to be used in respiration to release the energy needed to drive metabolism. The leaves are the organs of the plant where photosynthesis takes place. They are very effectively arranged and structured to make them suitable for absorbing light and getting carbon dioxide from the air. Also attached to the stem are the plant's reproductive organs, the flowers, which will be discussed in more detail later in this chapter. Below ground is the plant's root system. This serves two main functions, to absorb water and to anchor the plant in the ground. Near the ends of the roots are microscopic structures called root hairs and it is through these that water and dissolved minerals are absorbed. Root hairs function for a few weeks and then are replaced by new ones as the root grows.

Plants have many variations on this basic structure. Leaves can be a variety of shapes and sizes and can be arranged spirally, in pairs or singly along the stem. Stems can branch by having a main stem with side branches, or they may regularly divide into two. Some stems are horizontal, as in strawberry plants, and some can be underground (rhizomes), as in bracken, creeping buttercup and potato. Some root systems, for example the dandelion, are made up of a main taproot, which extends a long way down into the ground to collect water from deep underground. Others, such as grass, consist of many similar roots spreading out over a wide area. Weeds with taproots are difficult to get rid of as the root often snaps off and will eventually produce new shoot growth. By comparison, grass is easier to pull up – unless it has a creeping underground stem, when one plant seems to be connected to many others. Different parts of the plant can act as food stores and so become swollen. Many of these have become useful food sources for humans. Swollen roots include carrots, parsnips, radishes and swollen stems include potatoes, turnips, sugar beet and sugar cane. You can tell whether a vegetable is a stem or a root by looking for scale leaves and the leaf scars that are only found on stems. Potato 'eyes' are scale leaves. Some leaf bases can become swollen with food. Cut an onion in half from the pointed top to the bottom. You should be able to identify the triangular shaped stem that may have small shrivelled roots attached at the bottom, and along each side are layers. Each of these layers is a leaf base. A common classification of plant food sources is into fruit, nuts and vegetables. Roots, stems and leaves are vegetables. Fruits and nuts are the result of plant reproduction, and how this happens will be considered next.

## Plant reproduction

Plants are sexy! They are also able to reproduce themselves without sex. This **asexual** or vegetative reproductive strategy is very useful to humans because it means we can take cuttings and propagate plants and be sure of getting lots of identical plants. This means that the attractive or useful characteristics of the parent plant are retained. Such reproduction is generally fairly quick compared to the sexual process, and in the wild it enables a plant to quickly colonise an area where it is being successful. However, there are times when a plant is not thriving in the conditions it is in. The ability to produce variety in the next generation may mean that some of these new plants survive better than the parent. Some may not. But it is this **variation** that is important for the long-term survival of the species. Variation is the basis on which **natural selection** acts and is therefore the basis of **evolution**. Recognising variation and appreciating its biological significance is a key idea in understanding evolution and the world of living organisms. More detail about this is found in Chapter 5.

In considering sexual reproduction in plants, I shall refer only to flowering plants. A very simple classification of living organisms has two main groups, plants and animals. In the same way that there are lots of different types of animals, so there are lots of different types of plants. Children tend to use 'plant' as though it is synonymous with just one of these groups, the flowering plants, in the same way that they use animal as synonymous with mammal. Flowering plants are all plants that produce flowers, whether these flowers are large and showy, such as buttercup, daisy and rose, or small and inconspicuous as in cereals and other grasses or willow catkins. Some plants, conifers, produce seeds but do not have flowers. Other common non-flowering plants are ferns and mosses, but these do not produce seeds.

The basis of sexual reproduction is the same in all organisms. There are two different sexes, each of which produces special sex cells (gametes) that need to be brought together to fuse (fertilisation) in order to form the beginning of the next generation (the zygote).

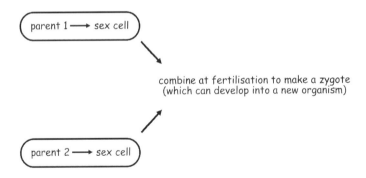

**Figure 3.2** The principle of sexual reproduction

Different organisms produce these sex cells in different structures: ovaries and testes in mammals, anthers and ovaries in flowering plants. Organisms produce a variety of different sex cells – from the swimming gametes of moss plants, sperm and eggs (ova) in humans to pollen and ovules in flowering plants. The mechanisms used to bring the gametes together vary, as does the way in which the zygote develops.

In flowering plants, the flower is the reproductive structure and, although some flowering plants produce separate male and female flowers, most contain both the male and female reproductive organs. This basic structure is not always clear in cultivated plants because these have been bred to be attractive. If you want to see the main parts of a flower, you need to select suitable flowers and, to show children, ideally ones that are as large as possible.

## Flower structure

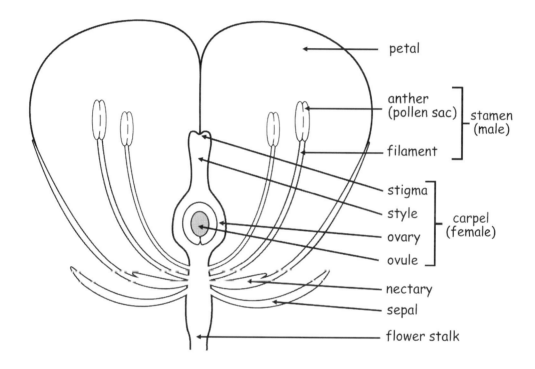

**Figure 3.3**  Parts of a flower

The flower is made up of several parts which each have a particular function. The sepal protects the flower bud. Together, the sepals make up the calyx. The next layer, working inwards, is made up of the petals. In insect-pollinated flowers, the petal is large and coloured to attract insects and has a nectary at its base. Inside the petals are the male reproductive organs. These consist of the anther, which produces pollen, and the filament, which positions the anther where it can distribute the pollen, either into wind currents or onto an insect. Together the anther and the filament make up the stamen. Note that *men* at the end of this word reminds us that it is male. The female reproductive organs are at the centre of the flower and consist of the stigma, which is sticky so that pollen remains attached, the style, which positions the stigma so it can receive pollen, and the ovary, which contains one or more ovules. Good examples in which to see these structures are buttercups and sweet peas. Once the basic structure is understood, it is then fun to explore other flowers and work out how they differ. Look at tulips to see the main sex organs, but note that the outer layer, the calyx of sepals, which protects the bud before the flower opens, is missing. In some flowers the calyx has a colour other than green and so looks like petals. Some flowers have several female organs made up of the stigma, style and ovary, while others have one central structure which may have several fused ovaries or only one. It is the difference in these structures that is used to classify different plant groups. The best way to see the structure of the ovary is to look at it after fertilisation, when it is called a fruit. It then becomes larger and easier to cut open to reveal its structure. A pea pod is much easier to investigate than the small ovary in a pea flower. Some flowers, such as clover and hogweed, are really several flowers all grouped together in one head. In some flowers the individual petals are fused together making trumpet or bell shapes, as in the daffodil. Once you are familiar with the basic structure, explore other flowers by pulling off the layers and identifying them – a sort of grown-up version of 'he loves me, he loves me not'!

## Pollination

The next question is how do the reproductive structures work? The anthers produce pollen and when they are fully developed, the ripe anthers split open and release the pollen. This pollen is either carried away by the wind, if the flower is wind pollinated, or by insects visiting the flower to feed on the nectar. Carried by the wind or attached to an insect, some of this pollen will end up in another flower of the same species and may then become stuck to the stigma. The transfer of pollen from the anther to the stigma is called **pollination**. Landing on a stigma of another type of flower means that the pollen does not develop further, but if it lands on a ripe stigma of the right type of flower, then it starts to grow. A tube emerges and grows through the style down towards the ovary. To enable this growth, it digests the style tissue, which both makes room for the growth and provides the energy needed. Once in the ovary, it grows towards a weak spot on the surface of the ovule and the nuclei carried in the pollen tube pass into the ovule and fuse with the female nuclei, and this fusion is fertilisation. The ovule is now called the seed and the ovary is called the fruit. These structures continue to develop and eventually the seeds will be dispersed (with or without the fruit) and some will settle where they can successfully germinate and grow into a new plant.

Pollination depends on pollen being transferred from a ripe anther to a ripe style. In order for the greatest variation in the next generation, it is better if the pollen from one individual plant is used to pollinate a different plant (cross pollination). However, it is possible that it will be transferred from one flower to another flower on the same plant or even be transferred within the same flower (self pollination). The advantage of sexual reproduction is that it produces variety and, because of the way the sex cells develop, even self pollination gives rise to a new mixing of the parent's genetic material, and so even self pollination is beneficial.

## Plant life cycles

A life cycle is a way of showing the developmental stages during the life of an organism. In some organisms, the stages are very distinct and look very different. Two good examples are the frog and the insect.

The frog life cycle is:

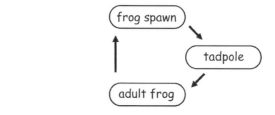

Insects either:

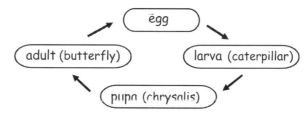

Or in, for example, the grasshopper:

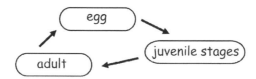

Plants also have a life cycle:

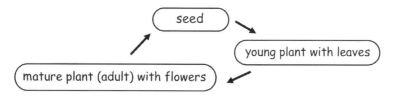

**Figure 3.4**   Life cycles

Within this life cycle are the processes of pollination and fertilisation already discussed. Once the seed has developed and been dispersed, it can then germinate to produce the young plant. This seedling begins to feed by photosynthesis, which enables it to grow and mature and so eventually produce flowers and new seeds. The seed contains the embryo plant and dried food reserves provided by the parent plant to enable it to germinate, a sort of packed lunch to last until it can make its own food! The seeds of many plants in our climate are adapted to remain dormant over the winter. **Germination** in the winter would expose the young seedling to harsh conditions, but mechanisms delaying germination until the spring or the best conditions for survival result in the seedling having the best chance of reaching maturity. In order for germination to occur, these food reserves need to be made readily available to the embryo. Water needs to be absorbed to dissolve the food and enable it to be carried to the growing regions of the embryo. Seeds also need oxygen and warmth for the increased metabolic activity that germination involves. In general, seeds do not need light in order to germinate, but there are some that are sensitive to light; some need light to germinate and others need its absence. Light is always needed for growth, because it is needed for photosynthesis. It is important when germinating and growing plants with children that the distinction between the two processes is understood. When starting with seeds, it is germination which is being investigated, not growth. To investigate growth, seedlings are needed and then it is possible to measure growth by measuring, for example, changes in height, the number of leaves, or by finding the change in wet mass.

## Nutrition in plants: photosynthesis

All living things need food in order to survive. When asked about the difference between plants and animals, most people would mention movement, some may mention colour. Biologically, the major difference between plants and animals is their method of feeding. Animals eat; plants make their own food. This process of making food is called **photosynthesis**. Many people who have learnt about this process during their secondary education associate it with an equation without really understanding what it means. All living organisms need to have a supply of carbon-containing organic molecules, carbohydrates, fats and proteins. The organisms that make these molecules are green plants and so plants occupy the bottom of the food chain and support all other living things, directly or indirectly. Eventually, food is used to release the energy needed to drive metabolism and keep things alive. So the important questions are where does the energy come from and how does it get into the food molecules?

## Capturing sunlight

The energy comes from the sun. Plants are designed to be good sunbathers, using their leaves to absorb the energy from sunlight. Leaves are arranged to minimise overlapping, are flat, thin and green. Plants that grow in shady conditions tend to have bigger leaves and to be a darker green. Some plants that grow on the floor of woodlands, such as bluebells, complete their growth and flowering in the spring, before the trees come into full leaf. Spring sunshine is not as strong as that in full summer, but for the bluebell, weaker uninterrupted sunlight is a good option. Despite being adapted to trap sunlight, leaves are not very efficient. You can see, or even measure using a light meter, how much light passes straight through the leaf. Even where there are several layers of leaves in, for example, woodland, there is still some light that reaches the floor. Plants trap about ten per cent of light reaching the Earth and it is on this that life on Earth depends.

## Using sunlight

It is the green pigment, **chlorophyll**, in the cells of the leaves that absorbs the light energy. This pigment is found in structures called **chloroplasts**. Chloroplasts are not static in the cells, but move around the cell so that their performance can be optimised. The 'packets' of light energy are used to join together two basic molecules, water and carbon dioxide. This results in a simple organic molecule, a sugar, being made. Breaking this molecule up later will release the energy trapped initially. The water needed is absorbed by the roots and carried up through the plant to the leaves in hollow transporting vessels. In the leaf, it leaks out to provide a wet environment and the steady supply of water needed by the photosynthesising cells. The carbon dioxide comes from the air. In order to get to the leaf cells, there need to be openings in the leaf. These openings are called stomata, but they have the disadvantage that water can also escape through them. This water loss is called **transpiration**. However, transpiration also drives the movement of water up through the plant and, providing there is not a water shortage, it is not a problem for plants. If there is a water shortage or water is being lost too quickly in windy conditions, the plant can close its stomata and stop photosynthesising until the situation improves. When plants shut down in this way, their growth rate is slowed down. Without food being made, growth cannot continue. Plants and crops that are not kept fully watered do not give good yields, and so we see crops being watered during dry summers and irrigation methods developed worldwide.

## Photosynthesis summarised

So, in summary, green plants use carbon dioxide, a gas from the air, and water, a liquid, in order to carry out a complex chemical reaction (which our technology cannot replicate!) that results in a sugar, a solid, being made. This sugar contains energy, originally provided by the sun, in a form that can be accessed by all other living organisms. Very complex chemistry is carried out without the noise and mess of a huge chemical complex. As with many industrial processes, there is a waste product. During photosynthesis the plant produces oxygen as waste. Very early in the development of life on Earth, it was this waste by-product that fundamentally changed the atmosphere and provided the conditions for life as we know it to evolve. Photosynthesis remains the fundamental process supporting life on Earth and as teachers, we need to appreciate both its significance and the awesome complexity of the reactions taking place in plants.

## Using minerals

Once sugars have been made, plant cells are able to use these to make other food molecules. Fats contain the same elements as sugars, and so sugars can be converted to fats by a chemical rearrangement. In order to make proteins, plants need other elements, especially nitrogen, and these are obtained dissolved in the water absorbed by the roots. Most plants are completely self-sufficient, but some fascinating plants have developed other ways of getting the nitrogen they need. These are the insectivorous plants, such as the venus flytrap and the sundew, which grow where there is very little or no nitrate available from the soil. They get the nitrogen they need by capturing insects and digesting them. Where plant growth is high, there may be a need to supply extra nitrogen, in the form of nitrates, to the soil. This use of artificial fertilisers is needed where plants are being removed or harvested each season. In natural conditions, plants would die and, as they rot, the nitrates would be released for use by the next generation. We may also need to add fertiliser to houseplants because there is too little in the compost in the pot. Although referred to as 'feeding' plants, adding fertiliser is adding minerals essential for healthy growth and is the equivalent of supplementing our diets with vitamin tablets. Plants lacking essential minerals show deficiency symptoms; most commonly, the leaves turn yellow.

## Common misconceptions

Defining living things using the life processes requires an understanding of each of the processes and of the organism. Decisions are usually made on the basis of general knowledge and a key life process, such as movement, or a simplification, such as breathing. Recognising the life processes in plants is therefore more difficult than in animals.

Many people do not understand the use of *plant* to mean a group of living organisms but use it synonymously with *flower*, or they use categories such as *plant* and *weed*. This imprecise use of the word also means that trees are not classified as plants, nor are grasses or mosses. In a similar way, a flower is thought to be the whole plant found in a garden and not just the reproductive structure.

The basic similarity between sexual reproduction in plants and animals and the benefits of this in producing variation is not understood. Plant reproduction is seen as a very different process. Self-fertilisation is confused with asexual reproduction. The important difference is that, by producing pollen and ovules, the plant produces seeds that contain a different mix of the genetic information and so produce variety in the next generation. An understanding of reproduction needs to place it within a life cycle that connects generations. Reproduction is not just producing babies or seeds; it is a stage in the life cycle that ensures continuity of the species.

Plants are commonly thought to feed through their roots – absorbing nutrients from the soil. Plants absorb minerals needed for health and make their own food. The role of carbon dioxide as a basic raw material for this process is overlooked and only considered in terms of gas exchange. Plants are incorrectly thought to be changing carbon dioxide into oxygen as a secondary reaction in photosynthesis. In fact, the oxygen comes from breaking up the water molecule. Plants get heavier because the carbon dioxide from the air is used to make solid sugar, which is incorporated into the plant structure. Plants are not made from soil.

## Review Questions

1  What are the basic differences between plants and animals?
2  How could you demonstrate that a plant is alive?
3  Where are the growing regions of plants, and what happens to them in the winter?
4  How do flowers have sex?
5  Why is photosynthesis so important?
6  How does the plant get the raw materials for photosynthesis, and what is needed to enable the process to take place?
7  Why do plants need minerals?

## Review Activities

1  Find out about viruses and why they may not be considered living things.
2  Using commonly eaten fruit and vegetables, try to identify which part of the plant each is and where it fits in the plant's life cycle.
3  Research human use of vegetative reproduction by artificial propagation of plants.
4  What are the differences between wind- and insect-pollinated flowers? Why would flowers evolve in this way?
5  Make a collection of seeds and fruits and consider their different dispersal mechanisms.
6  Find out more about unusual plants such as insectivorous and parasitic plants.

# CHAPTER 4

# The environment

## QCA Units

This chapter supports the teaching of the following QCA units:

- Plants and animals in the local environment
- Habitats
- Interdependence and adaptation

## National Curriculum

This chapter supports the following sections of the National Curriculum:

- Key stage 1 Living things in their environment
- Key stage 2 Living things in their environment

By reading and reflecting on this chapter, you should have developed your learning about the environment and be able to:

- Define key ecological terms relating to the environment and ecology.
- Be able to explain feeding relationships and use terms and diagrams to represent them accurately.
- Cite examples of feeding adaptations.
- Know of examples of adaptations as shown by a range of organisms and by different stages of the same organism.
- Plan effective ecological investigations.

- Have an informed discussion about environmental issues such as pollution, climate change and conservation, relating these to the need to protect our environment.

- Appreciate the complexity of the interdependent relationships between different organisms and between organisms and their environment.

## The environment and ecology

**Environment** is a commonly used term meaning everything 'out there' and, as such, lacks precision. More precise language helps us to organise our thoughts, and with such a large topic as 'the environment', it is helpful to define some key terms. **Ecology** is the scientific study of the environment. Ecologists study **ecosystems**. These are areas that they have defined and they can be any size, from the whole world to a woodland to a single tree. It helps if the ecosystem has a clear boundary, so that the area to be studied has limits. These limits can be artificial, such as a garden fence, or more natural, such as the edge of a pond or lake. Ecology involves studying both the living things and their non-living surroundings. The non-living area is called the **habitat**, the place where organisms live or their address. We can describe and often measure a range of environmental conditions such as light levels, temperature, moisture level, acidity, soil type, slope and prevailing wind. Identifying which conditions are most influential and relevant to the study is difficult, and when first working with children undertaking an environmental project, it is useful to try to identify the range of conditions and to discuss how these may affect the organisms found. All the living organisms make up the **community** and within this community are groups or populations of similar organisms (species). The organisms in an ecosystem are mutually interdependent. They require food, water, space and shelter and are in competition for survival and the opportunity to successfully reproduce. Over many generations, this competition for survival, the effect of natural selection, favours the survival of the best competitors and results in organisms that appear well suited or adapted to live in a particular environment. Such change over time, **evolution**, is discussed in more detail in the next chapter. How organisms affect each other and their environment, and how the environment affects them, is the basis of ecology.

## Feeding relationships and food chains

One of the most obvious relationships to study is how organisms feed. What eats what and how are the different organisms adapted to be successful food producers, hunters or prey that avoids being eaten? When we first start thinking about this, we tend to focus on the animals and think about what they eat. This leads to a simple classification of animals into herbivores that eat plants, carnivores that eat other animals, and omnivores that eat both plants and animals. Carnivores are also referred to as predators and the animals that they eat as prey.

## Food chains

In order to study feeding relationships, the complexity of animals having multiple food sources needs to be unpicked. Once this is done, feeding relationships can be represented in a diagram called a **food chain**. In a food chain only one food source is considered for each organism in the chain. So a rabbit may actually eat grass and strawberry plants and peas and beans, but in a food chain we would only think about one of these. We then consider the rabbit and what may be eating it. From this could come the food chain:

grass → rabbit → fox

but just as correctly the food chain could be:

pea → rabbit → human

In these diagrams, the arrow should indicate the direction the food goes because it is the energy and nutrients in the food that are being transferred from one organism to another. The names in the food chain do not represent individual animals, but populations of animals in a particular habitat. We can then look in more detail at one particular type of organism and build up several food chains, all of which have this organism in common.

## Feeding relationships

To describe the feeding relationships in the habitat, we can complete all the food chains for all the organisms. This results in a very complex interlinked diagram called a **food web**. What becomes apparent from drawing these diagrams is that organisms have a particular role and position within the chain or web. At the bottom or beginning of the chain is usually a green plant or part of a plant, such as a seed or leaf. These are called **producers** because, as explained in Chapter 3, these are the organisms that actually trap sunlight energy and transfer it to food molecules by the process of photosynthesis, i.e. produce food. The next layer is made up of the **primary consumers** (first eaters), which is a better term than herbivore because some of these organisms are omnivores, and so will be carnivores in other food chains. In the next layer are the **secondary consumers**, and there may also be a third or tertiary consumer layer. Common features of food chains are that they are short and the population size generally decreases the higher in the food chain the animal is. So there are fewer foxes than there are rabbits in the same habitat. If this were not true, the foxes would quickly eat all the rabbits and have nothing left to eat. Animals at the end of long food chains usually feed lower down other food chains and may feed on a wide variety of foods. The reason for this is that feeding represents the transfer of energy between organisms. All organisms need energy to maintain their life processes and so they use energy as they grow and move about. Some food is used to make the body structure and excess is stored as fat. When an animal is eaten, not all of the body can be digested and so the energy in these structures is not passed on. Calculations show that, as a result of each organism using some of the energy that they take in and with not all of the energy within the body being available to the next organism, only about 10–20 per cent of the energy at each level of the food chain is available for the next level. Food chains cannot be too long or the top organism is using more energy to capture and eat its food than is available from the food.

## Feeding adaptations

Finding, eating and digesting food is an essential part of living. It is essential that organisms are successful at getting food or they will not survive and be unable to reproduce. Finding food and escaping being eaten is therefore an important factor in the evolution of species. The result of this evolution is that the organisms we observe today appear very well suited or adapted to their environment. In Chapter 2 the different **adaptations** of teeth in carnivores and herbivores were described. Camouflage and warning colorations are also examples of feeding adaptations. Both predator and prey need to be able to merge into the background, and special colouring combined with behavioural responses such as staying very still or being part of a larger group can make it very difficult to spot some organisms. Even the stripes on a zebra that appear striking when viewed in Britain make more sense when these animals are seen in their natural environment with strong sunlight and shadows. Insects demonstrate another feeding adaptation. Within the insect life cycle different stages eat different foods. For example, caterpillars feed on the leaves of the plant using strong jaws to cut and chew the leaves, while adult butterflies feed on nectar and have long drinking straw-like structures that uncurl and reach down into the flowers and suck the nectar from the nectaries.

Caterpillars are abundant when the plants are producing lots of leaves; the butterflies emerge later after the plant has flowered. In a similar way, tadpoles feed on the vegetation in the pond and the adult frog feeds on flies and other insects when out of the water. These adaptations mean that adult and juvenile stages do not compete for the same food and so there is more chance of the young growing to maturity, particularly when food is not plentiful. When studying organisms in a habitat, it is helpful to think about why they are found in that particular place. Is this where they find food, or shelter? If I want to find organisms, I should look where their food is! Another question to consider is what structures help an organism hide from predators or enable it to hunt successfully? Herbivorous mammals often have eyes on the side of their head; this gives good all-round vision for detecting movement, but not great detail. Carnivores have eyes at the front; this gives them good stereoscopic vision, so they can judge distances – it helps to know exactly where your prey is when you pounce.

## Other common adaptations

### Seed dispersal

Plants are also adapted to their environment in many different ways. Being stationary, they have various mechanisms for dispersal. The seeds are carried away from the parent plant so that they do not have to compete for space, light, water and minerals. Different mechanisms are used to disperse fruits and seeds. Coconuts are buoyant and are dispersed by floating from one tropical island to another. Adaptations for wind dispersal include the winged seeds of sycamore and maple trees, the parachutes (or 'fairies') of dandelions and the thin floaty papery seeds of conifers. Animals are widely used. Cleavers stick to animals by means of hooks and sticky chemicals. With apples, the fruit is eaten and the seed thrown away or dispersed, and the tiny pips (seeds) in strawberries are eaten but pass through the digestive system and are then 'planted' with their own supply of fertiliser! Squirrels collect seeds and bury them and although some are collected during the winter, many are left nicely planted and may germinate the following spring. Some seeds are not dispersed far but are thrown from the parent plant by explosive mechanisms. Broom plants can be heard popping in the summer; the seed pods burst open and scatter the seeds as they split. Poppies have small openings in the top of the seed pod so that the seeds are shaken out as it is moved by the wind. Amazingly, moss plants have a very similar mechanism but much smaller; you need a microscope to look carefully at the pod-like structures that appear on moss plants. When ripe, these have an intricate arrangement at the top through which moss spores are dispersed.

### Water conservation

Plants also show interesting adaptations for water conservation. As discussed in Chapter 3, the leaves are the plant feeding organs, carrying out photosynthesis and making food. At the same time, water is lost from the underside of the leaves. To reduce water loss when water is in short supply and still be able to get the carbon dioxide from the air in order to photosynthesise, plants show a range of strategies. Conifers have reduced the size of their leaves to form the familiar 'needle' of pines, for example. This means there is less surface area from which water can escape and be lost. The leaves are also very dark green as they have more chlorophyll to compensate for the reduced area available to trap sunlight. The needles do fall from the tree but not all at the same time, so there are always leaves trapping sunlight for photosynthesis. In cacti, the leaves have become reduced to spines and the photosynthetic function has been taken over by the stem. This reduces water loss because stems have fewer pores in them through which water can escape. By being folded, leaves and stems create a humid environment next to the pores and this also reduces water loss. This effect is similar to trying to dry washing on a misty day.

## Evasion

Both plants and animals show evasion strategies. Deciduous trees in temperate climates lose their leaves in winter, when water cannot be absorbed from the frozen ground. This limits growth in winter but enables the tree to survive until the following spring. Over-wintering as seeds, bulbs and tubers are other ways in which plants are adapted to actively grow when conditions are most suitable. Similarly, some animals hibernate during the winter when food is in short supply. Evasion from very hot conditions is also shown; desert rats (gerbils) live in burrows or tunnels underground during the day, emerging at night when it is cooler in order to feed. Whenever we look at an organism's structure or lifestyle, we can begin to think about how a feature or type of behaviour enables it to survive. The organism has not planned this: it is just that, without these adaptations, the chances of survival are reduced.

## Ecological investigations

The organisms we find in different environments are there because they arrived by seed dispersal in plants and by birth or migration in animals. Animals may be searching for food, shelter, water, or a mate. They may have travelled long distances or be living in the same area as past generations if there is no pressure on the habitat to provide for all these needs. Species have optimum conditions in which they thrive and successfully reproduce. Having observed organisms in the environment and collected data about which species are found where and in what numbers, we can begin to look for explanations. So, having found lots of snails in our garden, we may have noticed that there were more on our hosta plants than on our holly bush. Is this because snails prefer the taste of hosta leaves? Setting up a choice chamber experiment enables us to test our ideas without having all the different variables present in the natural environment to consider. So we collect a sample of snails and put them in a suitable container at the right temperature and humidity and provide both hosta and holly leaves. If we record how many of each type of leaf is eaten, we can see if snails are more common on hosta plants because they prefer them. If both are eaten, the absence of snails on our holly bush must have another explanation. Perhaps the snails have not migrated that far or there is a barrier they cannot cross to get to the holly.

Whenever carrying out ecological investigations, it is important to have a reasonably large amount of data. It would not be reasonable to draw conclusions about the food preferences of snails based on one experiment with one snail. Similarly, in carrying out our initial search and formulating our hypothesis, it is important to have looked in several gardens and base our ideas on finding more than one snail. So, if you want to set simple traps, such as pitfall traps (plastic drinking cups buried level with the surface of the soil so that a crawling animal falls in and is captured), or look under stones in the school grounds, you need to look under lots of stones and set several traps to begin to get a picture of what sort of animals are usually found there. You also need to consider what other factors are having an effect. It is not possible to control all the environmental variables and have a fair test in which only one factor is different. This means that if you are comparing animals living under stones in a flowerbed with those living under stones on a footpath, you need to consider what the other differences are. There may be differences in moisture or the type of soil and, because these cannot be controlled, your conclusion needs to acknowledge that any differences found may also be influenced by one or more of these factors. It is useful to compare both the numbers of each type of animal found in different habitats and also the variety of animals. Remember that top predators may not be very numerous but they are significant.

## Environmental issues

There is a growing worldwide realisation that the environment is not an infinite resource that we can exploit and use as a giant waste depository. There are economic and political consequences of environmental policies and, as responsible citizens, we should have an understanding of this area of science so that we can enter into a more informed discussion. Some of these issues – conservation, pollution and global warming – will be introduced here.

## Conservation

Conservation is about saving or keeping plants, animals, and habitats for future generations. Fifty years ago the environment was perceived by many as something that could be scrubbed clean and preserved as it had always been. The natural process of change over long periods was often ignored with the general human population believing that the countryside of their youth was how it had always been and should be kept. Much of the British landscape is the result of human activity. Changes in farming practices and woodland management affect habitats and communities that live in them. Some of these changes – for example, removing miles of hedgerows to facilitate more mechanical and efficient food production and building motorways and other roads – have affected the diversity and distribution of plants and animals in our countryside. Conservation has a cost associated with it and keeping hedgerows would mean less efficient and more expensive food production. How much are we prepared to pay to keep the diversity of organisms and, in some cases, particularly rare or unique ones seen by only a small proportion of the population? We may have to compromise and conserve in one area and not in another. We need to understand our responsibility for the world in which we live and develop an appreciation for the wide variety of organisms, not just the obvious and 'cute' ones. We need to understand that what happens to one population can affect others and the environment. Change will happen, but we can work to manage the environment to keep those features that we find valuable and to reduce conflict between human needs and industrial development and the environment. By understanding more about the complex relationships between organisms and their environment, and our influences on them, we are in a better position to make what are difficult choices and compromises. We certainly need to know what is in the environment before we begin to destroy it.

## Pollution and human population expansion

The size of the human population is increasing and this has a big effect on the environment. More humans means that more food needs to be produced or captured, more clean water is needed for drinking, more space is needed for homes, industry and commerce, more resources are mined and more waste is produced. As we have developed and become more industrialised, so the pressure on the environment has increased. Using more water in our washing-machines and dishwashers means that more water has to be treated in sewage works; more packaging means more space is needed for refuse disposal or more incineration must take place. More cars means more exhaust emissions and increased demand for electricity results in more fossil fuel burning and consequent emissions into the atmosphere. Intensive farming has meant greater fertiliser use and a consequent effect on rivers and drinking water. The worldwide demand for oil results in it being transported across oceans and the occasional disaster when an oil tanker runs aground. We cannot turn the clock back, but by understanding what the effects are it may be possible to manage the effects of the human population on the environment so that the global ecosystem is not irrevocably damaged.

## Water pollution

Clean water is important for our survival. To ensure this, we need to monitor and control what is added to our freshwater systems. By using detergents and fertilisers, we increase the levels of nitrates and phosphates in our rivers and streams. Nitrates are necessary for plants to make proteins and so are readily taken up by water plants, including microscopic algae that are naturally found in fresh water. These plant populations thrive in the spring and summer when there is plenty of light for photosynthesis, and so take up the nitrates. Increased plant populations means there is more food for the primary consumers and so the animal populations can also increase. So far, adding nitrates to water seems to be beneficial. However, in the autumn, the plants begin to die back and decay. The bacteria and other decomposers that feed on dead plants are also able to increase in number, as their food supply is abundant. However, the decomposers use up oxygen and with vastly increased numbers the water system quickly becomes depleted of oxygen, which means that there is less available for other animals such as fish. Fish and other animals die and so fewer plants are eaten and the situation becomes worse. Without the added nitrates, there would be a natural seasonal recycling of nitrates; a take-up in the spring and fresh plant growth followed by decay and release over the winter, ready for the following year. The extra nitrates added by human activity can be incorporated into this natural cycle if they are not added too quickly or in too high a concentration. By understanding the effects of our detergent and fertiliser use, we can begin to find ways to manage it – not overusing fertilisers, reducing the amount of detergent used, improving sewage treatment and controlling the release of treated sewage so that these pollutants are diluted sufficiently to avoid oxygen depletion in rivers.

## Recycling

The increased pressure on space means it is not possible to continue to bury our waste in landfill sites. There is increased pressure to recycle and reduce unnecessary packaging. Many of us now have various containers for bottles, paper, metals and plastics that may be collected from our doorsteps and recycled. In towns and cities huge amounts of garden waste are included in household refuse and this can easily be recycled by composting. As in rivers, there are natural decomposers found in soil and these bring about the decay of dead plants and animals. By providing optimum conditions of warmth, oxygen and moisture, garden waste will be broken down into compost which, when spread on the garden, will return the important nitrates and other minerals that plants need for their continued healthy growth.

## Air pollution

Air pollution issues fifty years ago concentrated on particles in the air, mainly soot, which when mixed with fog became lethal smog. In December 1952 the London smog that lasted for a week is estimated to have killed 4000 people. The Clean Air Acts of the 1950s reduced smoke as a problem, but burning smokeless fuels still produces sulphur dioxide, a serious air pollutant. 'Scrubbers' in power stations have reduced emissions of sulphur dioxide, but it is still produced by domestic fires and car exhausts. In the air, this gas dissolves in any moisture to produce acids, which then fall as acid rain. This adversely affects plant growth, in extreme situations causing death. Another aspect of air pollution is the development of photochemical smog, a phenomenon well known in Los Angeles. It is the result of warm air being trapped near ground level and a build-up of gases from car exhausts, which react in the sunlight and warm air to form acids and low-level ozone, which are irritants and cause breathing problems.

## Global warming

Burning fossil fuels releases carbon dioxide into the air. The presence of this gas and others in our atmosphere results in a phenomenon called the greenhouse effect. This effect is essential for moderating the temperature fluctuations that result from the daily rotation of the Earth on its axis. When facing the Sun the Earth warms up; when facing away, it cools down. The atmosphere traps some of the heat and so acts as an insulating blanket, keeping the surface temperature of the Earth at an average 15°C, which is suitable for a wide variety of life. With no greenhouse effect the surface temperature would be about minus 18°C and life would not survive. The amount of carbon dioxide in the atmosphere is increasing as the amount that has been trapped in fossil fuels for millions of years is released when fuels are burnt. This means that the amount of heat trapped is greater, leading to global warming. Global warming has more serious effects than small increases in overall average temperature – it could lead to changes in sea levels as the polar ice melts, changes in weather patterns and climate. Global agreement is needed to manage the effects and control emissions.

## Interdependence and responsibility

After reading this chapter, you should have a better understanding that environmental issues are complex and important. We cannot scrub clean the environment but need to manage the human impact on it. We are one species and affect the environment in the same way as other organisms; the difference is that the environment does not control our numbers as we rely on technology to support our development. This means that our impact is potentially much greater. We compete with other organisms for food, shelter, space and resources and also rely on other organisms for the decay of our waste, for food, for producing raw materials such as wood, cotton, rubber, and we also use the environment for leisure and recreation. It is a valuable resource and we all need to understand our interdependent relationship with it. We need to be responsible for our impact on the environment both as a society and as individuals. If as an individual we throw our waste and litter into the local area, it is difficult to argue for recycling and pollution reduction at national and international levels. We need to learn to value the other organisms, and understanding their roles may help children appreciate the importance of the diversity of living things.

## Common misconceptions

The importance of photosynthesis as the basis of food chains, and the recognition that food transfer between organisms is actually a transfer of energy that originally comes from the Sun, is not understood. This means that arrows are drawn in the wrong direction on food-chain and food-web diagrams. It also means that while the dependence of animals on plants for food may be appreciated, the indirect dependence of animals on photosynthesis for food may not. Photosynthesis is more readily perceived as providing oxygen for animals. Feeding relationships can be thought of as the only way in which organisms are interdependent rather than just one of the ways in which they interrelate within a habitat.

Another common misunderstanding is that the organism at the top of the food chain eats everything below it, not just the organisms at the end of the arrow. The role of plants as producers in water ecosystems (both freshwater and in the sea) is often overlooked, particularly when the plants involved are microscopic algae.

There is also the egocentric and exploitative view of the environment, that it exists for the benefit of humans. Thus, other organisms exist to provide humans with food or resources, and this view is incompatible with the ideas of conservation and responsibility. This extends to ideas about pollution, which is initially understood as it affects humans rather than the wider effects on other organisms, particularly plants. A common misconception is that natural or biodegradable substances are not pollutants, that oceans provide limitless space into which things can be dumped. The human race is perceived as indestructible. Many people incorrectly link issues to global warming, such as using lead-free petrol and the depletion of the ozone layer.

## Review Questions

1 Check that you can correctly define key words such as ecosystem, habitat, community, population, producer and consumer.

2 Make up and draw a garden food chain based on dead leaves, earthworms, blackbirds and cats.

3 Label your food chain, producer, primary consumer and secondary consumer. What term describes the role of the cat?

4 List three ways that leaves can be adapted to reduce water loss.

5 Explain why fish die in heavily polluted rivers.

## Review Activities

1 Find out about the range of organisms found in two habitats and by researching feeding in some of these, construct simple food chains. Try a woodland or river setting. Think about what human activities could affect your food chains.

2 Create two imaginary organisms for a habitat. Make one an organism that would be successful and explain why. What effect would it have if introduced into the habitat? Create the other one with poor adaptations for this habitat and think about what could happen if it was introduced.

3 Go out and compare two areas in your local environment – for example a shrubbery with a flowerbed or a shady area with a more open area – and note whether there is the same number and variety of organisms. To begin with, you don't need to know exactly what each is, but you may want to find out more about the most commonly found organisms.

4 Research the work of conservation groups such as the Royal Society for the Protection of Birds (RSPB), Greenpeace and Friends of the Earth.

5 Monitor local and national newspapers for articles on environmental topics. What science questions do they raise?

# CHAPTER 5

# DNA and variation

## QCA Units

This chapter supports the teaching of the following QCA unit:

- Variation

It provides a background for all the biology units and key ideas supporting the understanding of current media coverage of gene technology and research.

## National Curriculum

This chapter supports the following sections of the National Curriculum:

- Key stage 1 Variation and classification
- Key stage 2 Variation and classification

By reading and reflecting on this chapter, you should have developed your learning about DNA and variation and be able to:

- Explain why variation is a key biological idea and know how to represent measurements of variation graphically.
- Describe the role of DNA in controlling cell function.
- Discuss the roles of sexual reproduction and DNA in producing variation within species.
- Link ideas of variation, mutation, natural selection and evolution to the diversity of organisms and their biological classification.

- Know the names and main characteristics of the major classification groups.
- Act knowledgeably and sensitively when discussing genetic syndromes such as sickle cell anaemia and cystic fibrosis.
- Read media coverage of gene technology, cloning and embryo research with greater biological understanding of the techniques being employed.

## Variation: a key idea

Variation, similarities, differences and classifying and grouping things are very basic human ideas and activities. We notice change; we learn to identify friends and family by spotting differences between individuals. We cope with the vast quantity of information about people and events by classifying or pigeon-holing them. Sometimes this leads to unfortunate stereotyping but, without the ability to group and classify, we would be unable to manage and make sense of the world around us. A good understanding of variation in biology is the basis for understanding biological classification systems and evolution. How this variation arises and can be explained in terms of our present-day understanding of basic biological molecules and genetics is the subject of this chapter.

**Variation** means difference. Among living organisms there are big differences between species because the amount of genetic material or **DNA** that they have in common is less than within species. Within a species there are more similarities and fewer differences because individuals have a lot of DNA in common. Individuals also develop differences during their lifetime in response to the environment. However, these do not affect the DNA and so will not be passed to the next generation. This means that if you take up bodybuilding and develop very large well-defined muscles, your children will not be born with large well-defined muscles, although it is likely that they will inherit the potential to develop this physique if they undertake similar training. Similarly, parents who become obese by overeating do not produce obese children, although since the children live in a similar environment, they may develop similar eating habits.

## Discontinuous variation

Within a species there are two sorts of variation. Discontinuous variation means that the differences can be put into categories. Two examples are blood groups, in which humans can be one of four groups: A, B, AB or O, and the ability to roll the tongue – you either can or you cannot and no amount of practice will enable a non-roller to master the technique. These discontinuous variations are the result of a single gene within our genetic make-up and are not affected by our environment. Within a group of people, a class of pupils for example, we can find out about blood group or tongue-rolling ability and record this information, initially as a tally chart. This can be represented in a bar chart with the different possible categories along the horizontal (*x*) axis and the numbers of individuals in each group on the vertical (*y*) axis. The bars would be separated, as there is no possibility of an intermediate category that would occupy the space between the bars.

## Continuous variation

Other variations can be measured and have any value along a continuous scale. Examples of such variations are height and size of feet. Feet can be any size if measured with a ruler – we just have categories for these, called shoe size. Several genes acting together and/or an environmental influence cause these variations. Simplifying the explanation, height can be thought of as the result of mixing together combinations of short, medium and tall genes and diet can affect whether we reach our potential height, because diet will influence growth. Measurements of continuous variation are often grouped; for example, heights between 151 and 155 cm, then between 156 and 160 cm, and so on, could be counted. These are then plotted on a histogram, with bars that touch, because the measurements are part of a continuous scale. Sometimes ranges of measurements are given values, such as shoe sizes, and again it would be correct to plot these on a histogram with touching bars.

Whenever we are looking at variation in the classroom, it is important to look at both similarities and differences and to develop a culture in which difference is celebrated, so that stereotyping and prejudice is not encouraged.

## DNA and cell function

Cells are the basic building blocks of living organisms. Within the cell is a dense structure, the **nucleus**, and this is surrounded by a complex chemical system called the **cytoplasm**. The nucleus contains strands of DNA (deoxyribonucleic acid), which are complex chemical molecules. In order for these molecules to be kept safe and be able to function properly, they are arranged in structures called **chromosomes**. Chromosomes are lengths of DNA held together with proteins. A very simple picture would be of very long pieces of thread (the DNA) being organised by being wound round cotton reels (proteins). Thus each chromosome is made up of a piece of thread and several reels. Humans have a total of 46 chromosomes in their cells.

## DNA and genes

The long thread-like DNA molecule is made up of sections that either carry coded information or are 'nonsense' sections. By far the greatest proportion of the DNA is nonsense. Each coded section is a **gene**. Each gene is a master copy of instructions that enables the cells in the body to make chemicals. These chemicals are either used to build structures or take part in the chemical activity, **metabolism**, which is essential for life.

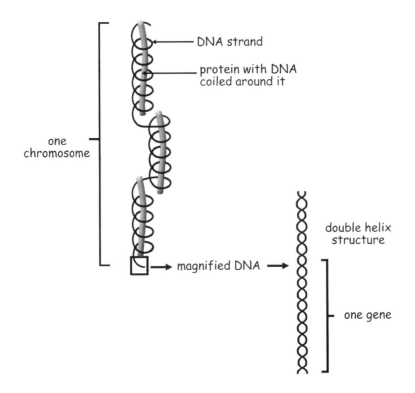

one
chromosome

DNA strand

protein with DNA
coiled around it

magnified DNA

double helix
structure

one gene

**Figure 5.1** DNA and chromosomes

By using different sections of the DNA (different genes), different cells can make a different range of chemicals and so can look and function differently. At the chemical level, we are the sum of a range of chemical reactions and so the genes ultimately determine who we are. Genes are the basic units of inheritance.

Having the coded information enclosed in the nucleus protects it from the chemical activity in the cytoplasm. Metabolism needs to be directed and controlled. To do this, instructions are sent out from the nucleus in the form of short-lived copies of individual genes. These copies can be replaced if the instruction is still needed. By determining which genes are copied and when, the nucleus controls the cell's functioning. Different cells use different genes and so, even though all cells contain the same full set of instructions, cells can be very different from each other. The genetic information in the nucleus can be thought of as a reference book which needs to be kept safe and the instructions as copies of particular pages. Muscle cells may use the instructions from chapter 6, say, but nerve cells may be using chapter 3.

## Sexual reproduction, DNA and variation

The instructions on the DNA need to be passed on to new cells. The body makes new cells in order to grow and to repair damage. When new cells are made, the DNA is replicated, and so each new cell has a full set of instructions and the same genetic make-up as every other cell in the body. The process of making new cells is called **mitosis**, and the way in which the chromosomes replicate and separate to ensure all cells have all the information is amazing but beyond the scope of this book. Mitosis results in all cells being identical to the original cell and to each other and is the basis of both growth and **cloning**. Cloning results in identical individuals and happens when reproduction takes place without sex. Plants commonly reproduce by this method. For example, spider plants grow identical baby spider plants at the ends of runners, as do strawberry plants. Reproducing in this way enables a successful parent plant to quickly colonise a local area. There is no need to find a mate and if the parent is successful, then identical offspring will also be successful. Recently, ways have been found to clone mammals by taking a cell and stimulating it to grow and divide in the same way as a newly fertilised egg.

More commonly in animals there is a mixing of genetic information during sexual reproduction. Thus we inherit some genetic information from each of our parents. If we received a complete nucleus from each parent, we would double the amount of DNA each generation and, apart from overfilling the cells, too much information would be confusing and unmanageable. In order for each generation to have a complete set of genetic information, a special nuclear division takes place in the reproductive organs. This division is called **meiosis** and the details are beyond the scope of this book. It is fascinating and amazing to think that because of this process each individual is unique. Each parent contributes half of his or her child's total genetic information. So that we don't receive the information for, say, making legs from each parent but no information about making arms, each parent actually contributes a complete set of information. A simple analogy is to think of the chromosomes as being chapters in a book of instructions about how to make a fully functioning human. Genes are instructions written on particular pages. We each have two complete books – one provided by each parent. Each book has 23 chapters, each representing a chromosome. This means that we have a total of 46 chapters or chromosomes in 23 pairs. Each chapter has the same number of pages of instructions representing the genes. When a human develops, the instructions are taken from either book and the use of, say, page 1 in book A does not affect whether the instructions on page 2 are taken from book A or book B. This means that we are the result of a mixture of instructions provided by our parents. Meiosis is the process by which the book we pass to our child is made by selecting a complete set of pages, arranged in chapters and taken randomly from the two books passed to us by our parents.

This analogy should illustrate the potential for variation through the process of sexual reproduction. We each pass on a new combination of information that we received from our parents. Each time a sex cell is made a different combination of instructions is possible; no two sperm or eggs are genetically identical. A different combination of parents results in different mixing, and this explains why there is still variation in populations of animals where there is a dominant male who mates with most of the females. Added to this, is the possibility of the DNA being changed randomly or mutating by the action of background radiation or inaccuracies in the copying process. Many mutations or changes to the DNA prevent it being able to function, but others have no immediate effect and some result in a change that may benefit the individual or their descendants. This new variation is the basis for evolution.

## Evolution and diversity

Understanding the theory of **evolution** depends on being clear about the starting points. The basic observations that the theory attempts to explain are that there is variation amongst living things and that much of this variation is inherited. It is also noticeable that in the wild, population numbers fluctuate but do not continue to increase. More offspring are born than survive to maturity. These observations lead to the idea that to survive to maturity involves a struggle for existence. Those that do survive are the result of a process called **natural selection**. This selection depends on how well individuals compete for the conditions that they need in order to survive, such as access to food, water, and space. Those that do survive to maturity have the opportunity to breed and their offspring will inherit their genes. Genes in those individuals that did not survive may be lost to the general population New variation occurs naturally as a result of sexual reproduction and mutation and so, over time, the loss of some characteristics combined with the inclusion of new variation, results in changes to the population characteristics.

Such change may be very gradual and pass unnoticed between generations but if you were able to time travel, the differences over hundreds, thousands or millions of years may be more apparent. Sometimes change occurs more rapidly such as when environmental disasters radically reduce populations. This may limit the number of variations in the population and the selection of a particular characteristic. Similarly, island populations evolve into distinct groups when compared with the mainland population because they start with a smaller range of variations and can be subjected to different natural selection pressures. Where generation time is short such as in bacteria, evolution can appear more rapid. Scientists seem to be engaged in a perpetual battle to develop antibiotics that the disease-causing bacteria do not quickly become resistant to. Antibiotics act to kill off most of the population but those that remain have a natural variation that is not affected and as these grow and multiply there is a new type of resistant bacteria.

## Diversity of organisms and their classification

As a result of evolution, there is a great variety of living things in the world. Where there is a lot of common genetic information, organisms look similar and have structures that enable them to be grouped or classified together. Cats are recognisable as a group although there are differences between lions and tigers. The smallest grouping is the species, a group that can interbreed. The smaller the amount of similar DNA, the more distinct the groups become. Cats and dogs are both mammals and have similarities, yet they are quite distinct from each other. Features that can easily be seen, such as fur, are used to classify organisms but biologists also use microscopic structure, chemical make-up and other characteristics.

Classification is a human activity and different people can devise different systems. A current and commonly accepted biological classification divides all living things into five main groups, or kingdoms. In the past we used just two – animals and plants – but some organisms do not fit neatly into either of these groups. The five kingdoms are: animal, plant, fungus, prokaryote and protoctist. The latter two group names are less familiar. Prokaryote means having no true nucleus, and bacteria are placed in this group. The protoctist is a group of organisms that don't fit neatly into any of the other four groups and it contains many aquatic single-celled organisms and the seaweeds.

*Animals* are mainly identified by their method of feeding, which is **heterotrophic**. This means that they eat other organisms. They also have some form of nervous co-ordination, and are made up of many cells which do not have cell walls, vacuoles or chloroplasts. A useful division of animals is into those that have a backbone (vertebrates) and those that do not (invertebrates).

Invertebrates include:

- *Worms* with soft bodies – for example, leeches, earthworms and ragworms;
- *Molluscs* with soft bodies and usually a hard shell – for example, snails, slugs, mussels, cockles, octopus, squid;
- *Echinoderms* with spines and five-way symmetry – for example, starfish and sea urchins;
- *Arthropods*, which is a huge group containing:
  - *Crustaceans*, distinguished by their large outer covering – for example, microscopic water fleas, and non-microscopic crabs, lobsters, crayfish and woodlice
  - *Millipedes*, with two pairs of legs per segment
  - *Centipedes*, with only one pair of legs per segment
  - *Spiders*, with eight legs
  - *Insects*, which have only six legs and are also a large and diverse group. They have interesting life cycles with different forms of the organism at different stages, such as nymphs, larvae and pupae.

The main vertebrate groups are:

- *Fish*, which are divided into two groups. Some have skeletons made of cartilage, a mouth on the bottom of the head and visible gill slits – for example, sharks, rays and skates. Others have bony skeletons, a mouth at the front of the head and the gills covered by a flap – for example, goldfish, salmon, trout.

- *Amphibians*, in which the adults are usually terrestrial, have a soft moist skin and lay their eggs in water – for example, newts, frogs and toads.

- *Reptiles*, which are mainly terrestrial but they have a dry skin with scales and lay their eggs on land. Examples are lizards, snakes, crocodiles and alligators, turtles and tortoises. Extinct reptiles include the dinosaurs.

- *Birds*, which are readily distinguished by the presence of feathers and wings. However, looking at their legs illustrates their similarity to reptiles.

- *Mammals*, which have skin with hair, usually do not lay eggs but give birth and feed their babies on milk. There are some egg-laying mammals in Australia (the spiny anteater and the duck-billed platypus) but, like other mammals, they suckle their young. The non-egg-laying mammals are divided into marsupials and the placental mammals.

*Plants* are distinguished by their ability to make their own food by photosynthesis, having cells with cellulose cell walls, a large central vacuole and chloroplasts. Plants include:

- *Mosses and liverworts*, which are mainly found in moist places. They do not have roots and they spread by means of spores, often produced in interesting and noticeable spore capsules.

- *Ferns*, which have prominent leaves called fronds. These have spore-containing structures on their undersides which, at the end of the summer, are well worth examining with a microscope.

- *Conifers*, which have cones but no flowers or fruits. The cones contain winged seeds that are light and dispersed by the wind. Conifers also have needle-like leaves. Examples are firs and spruces that are used as Christmas trees.

- *Flowering plants*, which are the most familiar of the plant groups and includes all our major food plants and those that we value for aesthetic reasons. They have flowers and seeds that are enclosed in a fruit. There are two main groups of flowering plants – the monocotyledons and the dicotyledons.

  - *Monocotyledons* have a seed that has only one main part, unlike the dicotyledon seed, which is easily divided into two. Consider, for instance, the difference between a single corn seed and a peanut, which separates into two parts. Monocotyledons also have leaves with parallel veins. Cereals and grasses are good examples but many common bulbs are also in this group, for example, lilies and tulips.

  - *Dicotyledons* have broader leaves and include familiar trees such as the oak, ash, beech and birch. It also includes shrubs such as roses and other wild and garden plants, such as buttercups, daisies, nettles, cabbages, pansies and geraniums.

*Fungi* are a group of organisms that feed by absorbing nutrients from other living things – either as saprophytes, which feed on dead and decaying material, or as parasites. Fungi include moulds, mushrooms and yeasts. Many parasitic fungi cause diseases, especially in plants, and so are of major economic importance. Farmers need to protect their crops against rusts and other fungal infections as they spread by means of microscopic airborne spores and lack of control can lead to serious consequences, such as the Irish Potato Famine, when a fungus was responsible for the loss of the potato harvest. Saprophytic fungi are important in bringing about the decay of dead organic material, important in the recycling of nutrients and in clearing away rubbish. Sometimes such decay is a nuisance – dry rot in our homes, for example. Yeasts are hugely important for brewing and baking – imagine a world without bread or alcohol!

## Genetic syndromes

We inherit both visible and invisible characteristics from our parents. As already stated, each of our parents has two copies of the total genetic information needed to make a human being. Each gene is present twice. There are only so many versions of each gene present in the whole population and each individual could have two identical or two different forms. What is known about the way genes act is that some of these versions are more likely to be used than others. Such versions, or **alleles**, are said to be **dominant**, and those alleles which we carry in our genetic make-up but which are not used are said to be **recessive**. Each human therefore carries a lot of unused genetic information and this may include some recessive variations that, if expressed, would cause illnesses. Equally, it may hold potential survival traits such as resistance to disease.

In some cases, recessive genes being sex-linked complicate the situation. Human males have one X chromosome and a much shorter Y chromosome. Consequently, some of the genes present on the X chromosome are the only copy available because there is no corresponding gene on the Y chromosome. This means that the allele on the X chromosome is always expressed in the male. Women have two X chromosomes and so have two versions of these genes. Sex-linked genes include those for colour-blindness and haemophilia.

## Colour-blindness

In humans, a recessive gene on the X chromosome causes red-green colour-blindness. If a man inherits this version of the gene from his mother, then he will be colour-blind. The man will inherit the Y chromosome from his father and this has no corresponding gene. So with only one version of the gene in his genetic make-up, this is the one that is expressed. A colour-blind man's mother is not usually colour-blind. She will have two versions of the gene and it is likely that the other one is the dominant version for normal colour vision. Such women are 'carriers' for colour-blindness. A minority of women will be colour-blind if they inherit an X chromosome from a colour-blind father and an

X chromosome from their mother that also carries the colour-blindness allele. This is far less likely than a man inheriting just one copy of the faulty gene. About eight per cent of males are colour-blind but less than one per cent of females.

## Haemophilia

Haemophilia is a more serious condition that can be explained in a similar way. It is also said to be sex-linked because it is found in men. The blood of haemophiliacs takes longer to clot than usual and so bleeding is more serious than normal, even in the case of minor knocks and wounds. The haemophilia gene is on the X chromosome and so a woman can have a normal blood-clotting function but carry the recessive haemophilia allele, which means there is a 50 per cent chance of her passing this on to her children. There is a 50 per cent chance that her daughters will also be carriers and a 50 per cent chance that her sons will have haemophilia. A mother has to pass on one of her X chromosomes and it is pure chance which one is in the egg. Queen Victoria is a famous example of a carrier. She had one son who was haemophiliac and two daughters who were also carriers.

For a woman to have haemophilia she would need to inherit the haemophilia allele from both her parents. As the gene is rare in the population, this would be very unlikely. Without modern medical treatments it would have been unlikely that any female haemophiliac would survive beyond puberty and the onset of menstruation.

## Other genetic syndromes

Cystic fibrosis, Huntingdon's, sickle cell anaemia and Duchenne muscular dystrophy are examples of genetic syndromes. In each case, the allele giving rise to the condition may be carried as a recessive gene by parents who are not affected by the condition. The chance of inheriting this version of the gene from one parent is one in two, and so there is a one in four chance of getting two recessive alleles if both parents are carriers. Inheriting both recessive forms of the gene gives rise to the condition. It is now possible to test samples of DNA to find out if you are a carrier. These genes are uncommon in the whole population and therefore there is a low probability of your children being affected. Where there is family history of the condition, genetic counselling is available to explain the consequences of having the test and the chances of future children being affected.

## Gene technology and biotechnology

Set up only 50 years after the discovery of DNA, the Human Genome Project was a huge international scientific collaboration to map the genetic make-up of humans. It began in 1990 and was completed in 2003 with a working draft available from June 2000. The aim of the project was to map the 50,000 to 100,000 genes present in human DNA by determining their sequence and function. The potential of this information to lead to personalised medicine has captured the imagination and support of the general public and stimulated biomedical research. It would be beneficial to be able to predict the effect of drugs on individuals and so be more exact about dosage. Knowledge of the human genome means that there is also the potential for gene therapy. There have been gene therapy trials, mainly in the USA, but this is not yet a common form of treatment. The understanding of genes and DNA has come a long way in half a century and there is still huge potential for both further understanding and developing ways that this new knowledge can be used.

Genome research makes a contribution to areas of molecular medicine that examine disease, drugs and gene therapy. Currently a research programme in Canada is transplanting insulin-producing cells into people with diabetes. It also contributes to microbiological research in disease detection, developing energy sources, environmental monitoring and in developing microbes to clean toxic waste. Forensic science, the development of crops that are resistant to disease, insects and drought and the breeding of healthier animals also benefit from genome research.

**Biotechnology** involves applying science and engineering to the use of living organisms or parts of them. It is not new. Brewing and baking are ancient examples of biotechnology. More recent developments include cloning and stem cell research. Within an ethical framework, new biotechnology techniques have the potential to benefit humans in improving our environment, improving health and healthcare. It is important that the biology is understood if we are to make a fair analysis of the risks and benefits and develop an ethical framework that provides the safeguards needed without hindering all research in this area.

## Genetic modification

Genetically modified organisms (GMOs) are not new. These organisms have had their genetic make-up manipulated. By transferring segments of DNA that contain specific genes from one organism to another, new characteristics are acquired by the recipient organism. Transferring genetic information within the same species is much quicker than traditional breeding methods because the outcome is more controlled. Transferring DNA between species enables new organisms to develop which would not have been possible with traditional breeding. Early examples of the use of this technique were the modification of bacteria so that they produce human insulin, used in the treatment of diabetes, and the modification of other bacteria to produce a range of antibiotics. The modified bacteria can be grown or cultured in large vats and because of the way the extra DNA has been inserted, the insulin or antibiotic is continuously being produced and can be extracted from the culture.

Other genetically modified organisms have not been generally accepted. In 1996 the first genetically modified food was being sold in the UK. It was tomato puree made from genetically modified tomatoes grown in the USA. The tins were clearly labelled and placed on shelves in supermarkets alongside non-GMO tomato puree. Additional information was provided via in-store leaflets and there were newspaper, magazine and radio articles about the product to publicise it. Three years later there was a campaign to oppose GM food. An initial impetus for this campaign was a small-scale study of rats fed on GM potatoes. This study, by Arpad Pusztai, was eventually published and remains controversial; its results were not widely supported by other researchers. Whether the research was flawed or not, it together with an active GM campaign has resulted in very little GM food being sold in the UK and the rest of Europe. The introduction of GM crops remains controversial. Some evidence suggests that these crops have an adverse effect on the diversity of other species, while other evidence suggests that these crops either have a beneficial effect on the surrounding environment or no effect at all. With indecisive findings, we are left with choices. For some the choice is a moral one; the idea of gene technology is either fundamentally wrong and humans should not alter the genetic make-up of organisms in this way or it is morally right to do so. For others the argument depends on views of what might happen in the future. What are the benefits and consequences? Within this debate there are a range of issues to be resolved. How are GM crops better? What crops could be accepted? Could GM crops be grown as animal feed but not for human consumption directly? What safeguards are needed and how should these be regulated or policed? What percentage contamination by GM seeds would be accepted in non-GM seed? What about imports and exports? These are not easy issues to address and resolve to everyone's satisfaction.

## Cloning

Animal cloning was first brought to the public's attention with the birth of Dolly the sheep. She was cloned from an adult sheep and so was genetically identical to her mother. The genetic material from one of the mother's cells had been transferred to an egg cell from which the nucleus had been removed. This egg cell was then stimulated so that it started to divide and develop in the same way that a fertilised egg develops. Once the embryo had developed sufficiently, it was implanted into the womb of the birth mother. Cloning is producing organisms that are genetically identical and is a technique commonly used with plants. In order to produce seedless fruits, it is necessary to produce new plants without any seeds. Producing identical plants by taking cuttings of stems, leaves and roots has been common practice by fruit growers and gardeners for generations. These techniques also enable hybrid varieties of, for example, fruit trees, using roots from one species and the shoot from another. An important difference with the technique used to produce Dolly is that sheep are mammals and so this raises questions about whether the technique would be possible with humans.

## Stem cell research

Stem cell research involves culturing special cells that are able to continue to grow and divide for a long time without becoming specialised. However, they can be triggered to become specialised into any of about 300 different kinds of cells. This research is trying to understand the changes that occur as cells develop. It also has the potential to grow specific cells to be used to regenerate diseased or damaged tissues, as in the treatment of Alzheimer's and spinal injury. Controversy centres on the source of stem cells. Stem cells from bone marrow do not seem to be controversial, but those isolated from embryos raise issues associated with the use of human embryos in research and medicine.

## Common misconceptions

Variation is often more obvious than similarities. It is often thought to be a response to environmental conditions rather than being linked to inheritance. The transmission of characteristics between generations is accepted and so it is expected that children will be similar to their parents. However, there are ideas that the differences are due to mixing of the parents' characteristics either as a sort of blending or because one sex has a greater influence. Thus boys inherit from their fathers and girls from their mothers or the male parent has a greater influence.

The chemical basis of genes and chromosomes is not understood. Genes are perceived as influencing factors, or 'parcels' of information, possibly without any physical structure. The link between genes and variation is either not made or poorly understood.

As variation depends in part on sexual reproduction, the distinction between this process and asexual reproduction needs to be made clear. Often sexual reproduction is used synonymously with 'mating' and this means that it is limited to humans and mammals. The ability of plants to produce variation through sexual reproduction is therefore overlooked. The environment is perceived as producing variation rather than acting on the variation that is already present in organisms. This misconception feeds into a misunderstanding of adaptation and evolution. One incorrect idea is that adaptation is a change made by choice in order to fulfil a future requirement; another is that variation is pre-planned rather than a natural feature of organisms. Adaptation is actually a response to environmental conditions and is only possible if the variation is already present. There is a need to distinguish clearly between the long-term adaptations of species based on inherited variation and the short-term lifetime flexibility shown by individuals but which is not inherited. This short-term variation may be a change in behaviour or the result of learning. What can be passed to future generations is a culture that values and transmits these skills.

## Review Questions

1  State three ways in which sexual reproduction gives rise to variation.
2  Think about variation in your own extended family. What family traits (similarities) are there? Why is variation so important to living things?
3  What would happen if all living things reproduced by cloning?
4  How would you distinguish a reptile from an amphibian?
5  What are the main non-flowering plant groups?
6  What are the main invertebrate groups and the main vertebrate groups?
7  How would you explain that evolution is not a development towards a pre-planned goal? Use the ideas of variation, natural selection, struggle for existence and competition.

## Review Activities

1  Collect details of maximum hand span and shoe colour and make suitable charts.
2  Find out more about how DNA communicates with the rest of the cell by finding out about the role of RNA.
3  Read more about mitosis and meiosis and use the internet to find pictures of cells dividing and in which the chromosomes are visible.
4  Find out about Charles Darwin.
5  Make a collection of pictures of plants or animals and arrange them according to the classification groups described in this chapter. Consider different ways to sort them.
6  Find out more about the genetic syndromes mentioned in this chapter.
7  Scrutinise the media for articles on biotechnology, GMOs, cloning and stem cell research. Are they being presented with bias? Is the science being explained?

# CHAPTER 6

# Classifying chemicals

## QCA Units

This chapter supports the teaching of the following QCA units:

- Sorting and using materials
- Grouping and changing materials
- Characteristics of materials
- Solids, liquids and how they can be separated
- Gases around us

## National Curriculum

This chapter supports the following sections of the National Curriculum:

- Key stage 1 Grouping materials
- Key stage 1 Changing materials
- Key stage 2 Grouping and classifying materials
- Key stage 2 Separating mixtures of materials

By reading and reflecting on this chapter, you should have developed your learning about materials and be able to:

- Explain the importance of exploring and understanding the material world and the objects in it.

- Classify materials by accurately using words that commonly describe the properties of materials.
- Classify materials into three states: solid, liquid and gas and recognise colloids.
- Develop an understanding of some basic ideas in chemistry, including atomic structure and bonding.
- Distinguish between elements, compounds and mixtures and describe techniques to separate mixtures.
- Explain that materials can be changed both reversibly and irreversibly.

## The material world

Before starting this chapter, it is important that you are clear about what I mean by *material* and *material world*. Material is not just fabric but all the 'stuff' in the world. This 'stuff' is also called *chemicals* and is the basis for the study of chemistry, in the same way as living things are the basis for the study of biology. Living things are also made up of chemicals and so the two areas of study overlap in an area called biochemistry. All chemicals originally come from the reactions that take place in stars; so the Earth has been formed from stardust and so have we. So what is this stuff and how can we begin to explore it?

We study the material world by grouping and classifying the materials we find. There are different ways of grouping stuff depending on our needs and the purpose of the study. This can be confusing sometimes if you attempt to match the language used in one classification system to the range of terms used when materials are grouped differently. Examples of such groups that will be considered in this chapter are: the periodic table, which organises the information about all the known basic chemicals; grouping common materials such as plastics and metals; and grouping by state into solids, liquids and gases. In order to understand the basis of these groupings, we need to understand what we mean by chemical properties, and it is interesting to relate this to chemical structure and an understanding of atoms and how they join together in different ways.

Although initially we explore the world around us using our senses, chemists also rely on a range of apparatus that can sort and classify matter more quickly and using properties that we can only measure and not sense. For example, mass spectrometers detect very small mass differences and so identify different substances, X-rays have been used in X-ray crystallography, which was important in elucidating the structure of DNA, and Geiger counters enable us to detect radioactive chemicals. Children will initially explore the material world using their senses, tasting and smelling and feeling objects as well as looking and listening to them. We need to encourage this exploration but make them aware of safety issues. Adults need to control the environment of small children so that they do not lick harmful substances. Babies naturally explore everything they come into contact with using hands, mouth and feet, but as children become more independent, they need to learn that some substances are harmful and should be explored with more caution. However, with care, supervision, guidance and health and safety training, children can and should use all of their senses to explore all the different materials that make up our world. Smells, texture, temperature changes, sparks, colour and colour changes are the exciting bits of chemistry we all remember. It is a fascinating world and once we begin to understand some basic chemistry, we may never look at 'stuff' in quite the same way again.

## Materials and objects

In investigating materials we need to distinguish material and object. The material is the basic stuff that things are made from. By shaping and treating this material in different ways, we can create objects. The basic material will have properties associated with it. For example, metals conduct electricity, and anything made from metal will have this ability whether it is shaped into a piece of wire, a spoon or a paper clip. However, the objects created also have properties of their own: metals can be found as wires wound to form springs or shaped as a spoon to hold liquid. These are object properties and similar objects made from different materials can share these properties. Spoons can be made from plastic or wood and still be able to hold liquid. The distinction between the object and the material that it is made from is important. This is sometimes made more difficult because of our use of words. Glass can mean the transparent material used in windowpanes, but it can also mean a drinking tumbler. Whenever we begin to think about how and why we use materials in different ways, we need to focus on the material. Try out some of the definitions in the next section by handling a range of things that you have collected together and think about whether you instinctively examine the object rather than the material it is made from. How could you make it easier to focus on the material?

## Material properties

In science, a *property* is a characteristic feature used to identify a material and distinguish it from other materials. It is not something owned by the material in the sense that we may own property such as homes or other possessions. Many of the words used to describe the properties or characteristics of everyday materials are in common usage and yet we often find it difficult to define the words precisely. We all have a sense of what *rough* means, but how do you explain rough to someone else without him or her experiencing it? Experience of these characteristics is important in understanding them, but it is also important to be able to use words with precision so that we communicate effectively. This section will provide definitions of some common words describing the properties of everyday materials. This should enable you to answer questions such as 'What makes this material different from that one?' more effectively.

## Elastic and plastic

One of the things we notice about samples of materials is that they have a shape. When describing the material to someone who cannot see it, we may say it is round, square or flat, for example. By handling the material, we may begin to investigate this shape and try pushing, pulling, squeezing or twisting it. Some materials can be stretched and when you stop pulling them, they return to their original shape. These materials are **elastic**. Good examples of elastic materials are rubber, polythene and nylon, found in objects such as rubber bands, balloons, carrier bags, and tights. Springs are good examples of elastic objects. You have probably noticed that these materials sometimes do not return to their original shape after being stretched. This is because materials have what is known as an elastic limit, a point at which the material is permanently changed in shape. Stretch a little and things spring back, but stretch too much and they do not. Up to the elastic limit, the amount of stretch increases in proportion to the amount of pull; double the pull and you double the stretch. Try this for yourself by hanging up a pair of tights and adding equal weights and measuring the amount of stretch. Stretchiness also depends on the thickness of the material; thinner materials stretch more easily and also lose their shape more easily.

When a material is permanently stretched, it is described as **plastic**. Good examples of plastic materials are pottery clay, pastry, plastics and metal. Such materials can be shaped to make a wide variety of different objects and so they are familiar to us. We have pottery plates, cups, jugs and ornaments, plastic containers, surrounds to our computers and TV, metal saucepans, cutlery and cars. Materials that are very plastic and can be shaped in this way are **ductile**. Not all materials can be stretched and there are other properties to consider, such as differences in appearance. Materials may be different colours, some are **shiny** and reflect light, some are **transparent** because light passes through them, and others are **opaque** because it does not. There is more about these properties in Chapter 11.

## Texture

The feel of a material is its texture. In some materials the texture depends on the size and hardness of the grains that make it up; sandpaper comes in a range of grades from smooth to rough, depending on the size and type of sand on the paper. Smooth means without lumps, so that it is easy for things to slide. Rough means having an uneven, coarse surface. Sharp means having edges or points that are able to cut or puncture other objects. Abrasive means that it will wear away other surfaces if rubbed against them. A material that is soft is easily deformed, scratched or dented and is also smooth and not sharp.

## Density

When handling materials, we also make judgements about 'heaviness' or 'lightness'. It is possible to weigh materials, but obviously the weight would depend on how much of the material we put on the scale. Intuitively, our feeling of heaviness or lightness is a measure of **density**. What we are judging is whether material is heavy for the amount or volume we have. Scientifically, density is calculated by dividing the mass in kilograms by the volume in cubic centimetres. In everyday life, we make similar judgements by comparing the heaviness of two pieces of material of the same size. When not thinking, when asked which is heavier, a kilogram of feathers or a kilogram of lead, we may reply the lead. Obviously, they weigh the same but lead is denser. Objects and materials that are less dense than water will float. Good examples are oil and most types of wood. Dense materials, such as steel, can be made to float by creating objects from them that occupy a large volume.

## Strength

A **strong** material is one that is difficult to break. To test strength, we use a force, a push or a pull. Some materials are strong when pulled and are said to have **tensile** strength, others are strong when pushed and have **compressive** strength. Nylon and metal have good tensile strength and are used to make objects such as ropes, wires, chains and cables. The strength of the tensile material increases with thickness; a circular rope four times as thick will be 16 times stronger. Materials with compressive strength include concrete, stone and brick. These materials are used for building because when piled on top of one another, they do not get squashed. Some materials have both good tensile and good compressive strength. Such materials are flexible because they do not break as they are pushed and pulled. Wood can show these properties when made into shelving. Piling heavy books onto a shelf can make it bend but not break. As the shelf bends the top part of the shelf is being squashed or compressed and the bottom part is being stretched or put under tension. A stiff or **rigid** material is not flexible and resists a change in shape. It will break more easily than a flexible material.

## Hardness

A **hard** material is difficult to scratch or dent. Members of some groups of materials, such as wood, have different degrees of hardness. There are hard woods, such as mahogany, and soft woods, such as pine. Similarly, some plastics are hard and others are soft. There is a hardness index that gives a maximum value of 10 to diamond. Diamonds cannot be scratched or dented by other materials. Steel has a value of between 7 and 5 depending on the type of steel, glass has a value of 5.5, tin a value of 1.5 and wood a value between 3 and 1 depending on the type of wood. Soft materials are easy to scratch or dent. Chalk is obviously softer than slate because when you rub chalk on slate, it wears away the chalk leaving a mark on the slate. Some materials, such as slate, are described as hardwearing. These are materials that do not wear out when rubbed. Many natural materials, such as cotton and wood, are not very hardwearing because, in natural circumstances, they would be replaced by new growth if worn away. Close packing of materials improves the hardwearing quality of objects. This is why steamrollers are used in roadmaking. **Tough** materials are not easy to break. The opposite is **brittle**, and such materials crack or break easily. Mixing materials together to make objects is another way of influencing their properties. Many of the objects we use in everyday life are made of more than one material and so show a combination of properties. Concrete bridges are made tougher by being reinforced with steel rods. The concrete on its own is brittle when stretched but the steel rods prevent this happening. Changing the material's shape – for example, by folding or corrugating – makes it stronger.

## Solids, liquids and gases

Another way of grouping or classifying materials is dependent on their state; are they solid, liquid or gas? It is important to understand that state is not fixed. All materials can exist in all states, dependent on temperature and pressure. We only observe some materials in one state because we don't commonly see things at very high or extremely low temperatures and pressures. Like many other groupings, this classification is not perfect and there are some materials that do not fit neatly into one of the groups. Typical characteristics of solids, liquids and gases will be given and then the exceptions will be discussed.

Solids are generally recognised because they have a definite shape and keep it. They are difficult to compress and therefore relatively strong. They are also dense. A common error is to think of solids as hard, but it is possible to have a soft solid, such as chalk. Liquids, which have no definite shape and can flow, are also difficult to compress and are dense. Gases have no definite shape and expand to fill whatever space they are in, and they are easily compressed and have a low density. Fill balloons with air or water and make ice balloons and try to squash them to see the difference. Thinking about syringes and water pistols illustrates that liquids are difficult to compress; neither of these would work if liquids could be squashed. Particle theory, discussed in the next chapter, provides an explanation of the properties of solids, liquids and gases.

## Colloids

If you choose to look at the right materials, it is really easy to use the solid, liquid, gas classification. However, many common materials do not fit so easily. Where would you put smoke, jelly, whipped cream or rubber? You may choose a 'best fit' or decide that these materials fit in an intermediate group because they show features of more than one state. The reason for this is that these are examples of colloids. A colloid is a **mixture** in which one of the components remains as tiny particles spread throughout the mixture. Sometimes we can make temporary mixtures by stirring solids that do not dissolve, such as flour, into water, but the flour particles will eventually settle out. In a colloid this settling does not occur. Although some colloids are solid mixed with liquid, it is possible to have other combinations, such as liquid in solid, gas in liquid, solid in gas, and so on. Many manufactured materials are colloids because they provide useful combinations of properties. This means that when sorting materials into solids, liquids and gases, it is very useful to introduce overlapping categories.

Smoke is a good example of a solid-in-gas colloid. Looking at smoke in a beam of light enables the tiny particles that make up the smoke to be seen; they are floating and moving randomly in air and do not separate out. If they did, cigarette smokers would end up with a lap full of smoke particles! Small dust particles behave in the same way. When liquids are spread in a gas, they form aerosols. Cans of air freshener and hair spray are able to form aerosols in the air once they are used. Mist and clouds are other good examples of aerosols. Clouds are mainly air with small water droplets in them. Where gas is spread in a liquid, foam is formed. Good examples are whipped cream, shaving cream, bubble baths, foam from a fire extinguisher and the head on a glass of beer. The difference between foam and an aerosol depends on whether the liquid or the gas is the main constituent.

Some liquids disperse in other liquids to give us emulsions. Common examples are milk, which is made up of tiny liquid fat droplets in water; emulsion paint, in which the colour is mixed in water; and mayonnaise, in which egg yolks and oil are mixed. When liquids are spread in a solid, we get a gel, of which the most common example is jelly. The relative amount of water and gelatine in the jelly can make it appear more or less runny and so more solid or more liquid. Gases spread throughout solids make the solid much less dense. Pumice is a natural air-in-solid colloid. Polystyrene is a good example of a synthetic colloid. Introducing air into a solid gives good insulation properties. It also makes the solid light and easy to handle, but retains the strength associated with solids and so makes a good packing material. A loaf of bread is another example of this sort of colloid. Having the gas trapped in it makes it easy to squash, so it does not behave as expected if classified as solid. Solid-in-solid colloids are also possible. Pearl gets its colouring from the mix of small particles that it contains.

## Atoms and molecules

All substances are made up of tiny particles and the smallest of these that has all the properties of a larger sample is an **atom**. Atoms are made up of even smaller particles and there are different models of atomic structure that help us to visualise, explain and predict how materials behave. In the simplest model of atomic structure, the atom is visualised as a sphere with a central area called the **nucleus** and outer areas called shells or orbits. The nucleus contains small particles called **protons** and **neutrons**. The outer area contains **electrons**.

These sub-atomic particles are given a mass relative to each other. The protons and neutrons each have a relative mass of 1 and the electrons are so much smaller that, compared to the other particles, their mass is negligible. What is important about electrons is that they have a negative charge. The atom as a whole has a neutral charge because the number of negatively charged electrons is balanced by the same number of

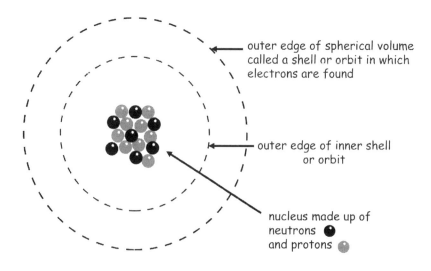

**Figure 6.1** Atomic structure

protons, each of which has a positive charge. In whole atoms the total mass depends on the total number of protons and neutrons. Some atoms, such as those of hydrogen, are very light because they have no neutrons and only one proton. Others, such as those of lead, are very heavy because they have 82 protons and over 100 neutrons. This gives hydrogen and lead very different properties; hydrogen is much less dense than lead and is a gas at room temperature, lead is a solid. Each type of atom has a different number of protons and it is the number of protons that identifies each atom. For example, carbon has six protons and oxygen has eight.

The electrons are important when atoms join together. In our simple model of the atom, the electrons can be visualised as incredibly small particles in constant motion. Their movement is within defined volumes, the shells or orbits in our model. Imagine that around the central nucleus there are concentric volumes. In the innermost layer only two electrons are able to orbit, but as the layers get bigger and further from the nucleus so more electrons can be found. Because the nucleus has a positive charge it attracts the negative electrons and prevents them moving beyond the orbit, and because the electrons are moving about, they do not fall into the nucleus, so a sort of stalemate exists.

Atoms join together to form **molecules**. Very few materials are made up of atoms that are not joined to other atoms. In most materials atoms are joined together to form molecules. One of the few atomic materials is neon; if you were to have a container full of neon and you could see individual particles within it, you would see neon atoms. However, if you had oxygen or hydrogen in your container you would see atoms linked in pairs, making molecules. So how do atoms join together? They join by forming **bonds** and three types of bond will be considered here – ionic, covalent and metallic.

Bonding

a) Ionic

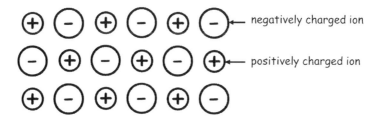

Pattern repeats in three dimensions

b) Covalent

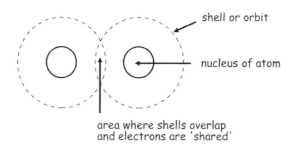

c) Metallic

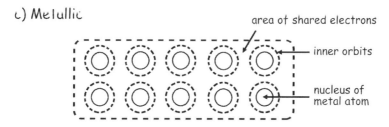

**Figure 6.2**   Types of chemical bonding

Ionic bonds form between atoms that have either lost or gained electrons. Some atoms are able to fill their outer orbits by taking electrons from other atoms. Other atoms readily give up electrons. Full orbits increase the stability of atoms and so there is a tendency for this to happen. When electrons are lost or gained, the atoms are no longer neutral and are known as ions. Atoms receiving electrons have a negative charge while those losing electrons have a positive charge. Materials that are chemically very reactive have this ability to give or receive electrons. When these chemicals are mixed together, this movement of electrons occurs and the oppositely charged ions that form are then attracted to each other and so 'stick' together. This sticking together is the ionic bond. The new materials formed are called salts. Common salt, sodium chloride, is a good example and is formed when sodium ions combine in this way with chlorine ions. The charged ions are held together in giant crystal lattices. These have a regular structure in which the positive and negative ions alternate in three dimensions. Ionic materials are hard and solid because of this regular arrangement. They readily dissolve in water because the water molecules are able to separate the ions and hold them dispersed throughout the water. Ionic materials also have high melting points because a lot of energy is needed to break the three-dimensional ionic bonds.

Covalent bonds are formed when atoms neither completely give up nor receive electrons. This type of bonding can be pictured as atoms being close together so that they share electrons. Some electrons are able to move in the outer orbits of more than one atom. Each atom gets increased stability because its outer orbit appears full. This bonding leads to discrete molecules being formed. The joining of the individual atoms to each other is very strong, but there is no strong attraction between the individual molecules and they are able to move independently of each other. The materials that are formed in this way tend to be liquids and gases because of this independence. A good example is methane, a gas formed when hydrogen and carbon combine.

Metallic bonding enables metals to form giant covalent structures. The individual atoms are arranged in a regular crystalline way but share some outer electrons to such an extent that these electrons can be pictured as being in a sea or cloud on the surface of the metal. This structure with 'loose' electrons gives metals their properties. The regular structure means that light is reflected, making metals shiny or **lustrous**. Having atoms close together makes metals good conductors of heat. Metals are described as **sonorous**, meaning that they make a ringing sound when struck. This is because sound is conducted between the closely packed atoms. The electrons on the surface are relatively free to move and this property enables metals to conduct electricity. Electric current is a flow of electrons around a circuit. Materials without electrons free to move in this way do not conduct electricity. Metals are also ductile (they can have their shape changed) and malleable (they can be pulled into wires) because the layers of atoms are able to slide over one another. Remember that in ionic materials the ions are fixed in place in three dimensions, while in covalent materials the molecules are not so close together.

## Elements, mixtures and compounds

So far we have considered different ways of classifying materials by using their properties, their state and by looking at their atomic and molecular structure. A different way of classifying materials is into groups called elements, compounds and mixtures. In this section the distinction between pure and impure substances will also be made clear.

**Elements** are the basic materials or building blocks from which all other materials are formed. There are just over 100 different elements and each of these elements appears in the periodic table. The periodic table is a summary of basic chemical information. Once understood, it reveals the structure of the atoms that make up each element, indicates relative reactivity and classifies elements into groups and periods. At a much simpler level, it provides a list of all the known elements – for example gold, lead, oxygen, carbon and nitrogen. Some elements, such as radium and uranium, are radioactive and dangerous to handle. Others, such as argon and neon, are very inert or unreactive. A useful division of the elements is into metals and non-metals. Ionic bonds form between reactive metals and reactive non-metals.

**Compounds** are formed when different types of atoms join together. It has already been stated that atoms join together to form molecules. It follows that all compounds are molecules. However, not all molecules are compounds. Some molecules are formed when atoms of the same element join together. Examples are oxygen and nitrogen, elements that exist naturally as molecules and not as atoms. Other molecules are formed when different atoms join together. Water is made from hydrogen and oxygen atoms, common salt is made from sodium and chlorine. Compounds have their own properties and are new materials. If you think of atoms as being like the letters of the alphabet, then compounds are the words. The number and arrangement of the letters determines which word is made; *lope* and *pole* have the same letters arranged differently and mean different things, *lot* and *loot* differ in the number of Os and have different meanings. Similarly, changing the number or arrangement of the atoms in a compound results in a different substance with different properties. Using over 100 different atoms enables a huge variety of different chemical compounds to be produced. When a particular compound is formed, the elements join in a fixed ratio. Water is made up of twice as much hydrogen as oxygen and this 2:1 ratio is shown in the chemical formula for water, $H_2O$, where H is the symbol for hydrogen and O the symbol for oxygen. Can you work out the ratio of sodium (Na) to chlorine (Cl) in sodium chloride, given that the symbol is NaCl? A more complicated challenge would be calcium carbonate, or chalk, which can be written as $CaCO_3$. The ratio is 1 calcium: 1 carbon: 3 oxygen.

A different way in which elements or compounds are found together is as a **mixture**. In a mixture, the materials are not chemically combined and the properties of the original chemicals remain; there are no new properties. Mixtures can have different proportions of each material in them. If you mix sulphur, which is a yellow powder, with iron filings, the iron is still magnetic and the powder is still yellow but may look 'dirty', depending on how much sulphur has been put into the mixture. Joining them chemically produces iron sulphide, which is neither yellow nor magnetic.

## Separating mixtures

Importantly, because the materials are not chemically combined in mixtures, it is possible to separate them. In the case of iron and sulphur, a magnet can be used to separate the iron, leaving the sulphur behind. If solids with different-sized particles are mixed, sieving can separate them. Soil is a mixture of particles; from the smallest to the largest these are: clay, silt, fine sand, coarse sand and gravel. Using sieves of different mesh sizes can separate the different particles. An alternative way is to mix the soil with water and then leave the soil to settle out; the larger, heavier particles will settle to the bottom first and the lighter particles will settle later, forming a top layer. The relative proportion of these particles determines what sort of soil it is; soils containing a higher proportion of the fine particles are generally more suitable for plant growth. The same sieving or settling techniques can be used to separate other mixtures of solids, provided that the particles are sufficiently different in size.

Adding water and then filtering can separate a **soluble** solid. The filter will trap the **insoluble** solid and the soluble one can be reclaimed from the solution by evaporating the water. Filtering is simply sieving but using a very fine mesh. Where more than one substance is dissolved, then chromatography can separate them. This technique separates substances depending on their relative solubility. Try this for yourself by using a water-soluble marker pen, black for an interesting result, and making a concentrated dot of ink about two centimetres from the end of a strip of blotting paper. Place the paper in about one centimetre of water. As the blotting paper soaks up the water, the ink will dissolve in the water and be carried up the paper. The most soluble ink colours will be carried the furthest and so you should find a range of colours produced on the paper. Try mixing coloured inks or food colouring and then separating them in this way.

Heating can separate mixtures of liquids. Different liquids boil at different temperatures and so heating the mixture, and then collecting and cooling the vapour produced at different temperatures, can separate the liquids. This process is called fractional distillation. The fractions are the liquids produced at each temperature and distillation is the name given to the process of evaporating and then cooling so that the vapour condenses. This process is used in distilleries to increase the alcohol content in drinks to produce spirits, and also in refining crude oil to produce a range of useful materials, including diesel and petrol.

## Purity

Whether you have classified a material as an element or a compound, it is possible for it to be pure. A pure substance is one that only contains one type of material; it is not contaminated or mixed with anything else. Pure substances are rare and if we want a pure sample then it needs to be completely separated and purified. Pure substances are generally expensive and for most uses not necessary. The salt we buy from the supermarket to put on our food is a mixture, we don't need 100 per cent pure salt for this purpose and some of the 'impurities' have been added to enable the salt to flow more freely.

## Reversible changes

When elements react, new substances are formed. However, there are changes that materials undergo where no new material is made. These changes are called physical changes, and they are reversible. The material is not chemically different and so it is able to react in the same way with other chemicals even though its external appearance may have changed. A bent or cut-up piece of magnesium ribbon still burns brightly if exposed to a flame. Examples of reversible changes are making mixtures, dissolving, changing state, expanding, contracting, bending and stretching.

## Common misconceptions

Some of the common misconceptions about material properties are the result of imprecise use of language. Confusing material with fabric, or confining a definition of material to a particular type of material, such as building material, are common errors. Similarly, not distinguishing material from the object leads to a confusion of properties. It can be difficult to distinguish properties that are associated with the material from those of the object. Looking at a range of objects made from the same material and the material in its natural state can help. Other confusions include distinguishing natural from manufactured materials. Natural materials are produced by plants and animals or are naturally occurring minerals. Natural materials such as wood can be shaped and treated to make manufactured objects. Other examples of incorrect language use include thinking and describing solids as hard rather than difficult to compress, and using *pure* to mean safe and not harmful rather than made of only one kind of material.

Children ignore some materials such as gases, including air. Air is 'nothing', and gas is not a general term but specific to that used for cooking and heating in our homes. Weighing air is problematic. The simple use of a filled balloon on a balance gives a good result for all the wrong reasons. It weighs more than an empty balloon because the air in it is denser because the elastic nature of the balloon squashes it!

Atomic theory and the structure of the atom are often incompletely understood. The idea of nothing existing between atoms in a solid and of nothing existing between the sub-atomic particles is challenging. Often, atoms are perceived as having the same properties as solids and are incorrectly thought of as hard or coloured. The use of relative mass to describe the sub-atomic particles can be confused with actual mass. It is not uncommon for people to think that a hydrogen atom has a mass of one gram rather than a relative mass of one when compared with other atoms. For an explanation of the difference between mass and weight, see Chapter 10.

Mixtures and compounds are confused and the importance of elements combining in a fixed ratio to form compounds needs to be understood. The variation in the properties of mixtures that arises from having different proportions of the constituents is often overlooked.

## Review Questions

1  Why is it important to distinguish material from object?

2  What is the difference between elastic and plastic, between hard and soft and between tough and brittle?

3  Explain why an understanding of colloids is important when identifying states of matter.

4  How are molecules different from atoms?

5  In what different ways can atoms combine together?

6  Distinguish between element and compound and explain what is meant by pure substance.

## Review Activities

1  Use the material property definitions given in this chapter to describe a range of materials, such as wood, plastic, aluminium, and wool.

2  Look at the materials in your desk or bathroom cabinet and decide if they are solid, liquid or gas. What other categories do you need to use?

3  Find out about hydrogen bonding and explain why ice is less dense than water.

4  Use the internet to find out more about the periodic table and the different elements.

5  Try out the different separation techniques described in this chapter.

# CHAPTER 7

# Chemical properties and kinetic theory

## QCA Units

This chapter supports the teaching of the following QCA units:

- Solids, liquids and gases and how they can be separated
- Gases around us
- Changing state
- More about dissolving

## National Curriculum

This chapter supports the following sections of the National Curriculum:

- Key stage 1 Changing materials
- Key stage 2 Grouping and classifying materials
- Key stage 2 Changing materials
- Key stage 2 Separating mixtures of materials

By reading and reflecting on this chapter, you should have developed your learning about materials and be able to:

- Describe the kinetic model and use it to describe the behaviour of particles in solids, liquids and gases.
- Explain changes of state in terms of the behaviour of particles.
- Use the model to explain dissolving.

- Use your understanding of the model to explain diffusion, expansion and pressure.
- Apply your understanding of change of state to the water cycle.

## The kinetic model

Science is about trying to explain things that happen in the world around us. Sometimes models or theories have been developed which provide an explanation and enable predictions about other situations to be made. Some of these theories have been around for a long time and have been found to be very robust and useful. One such theory is the kinetic theory. It provides a model to explain how materials behave in a range of conditions. This theory starts with four basic ideas. These are that:

- all materials are made up of very tiny moving particles;
- particles in different substances have different masses;
- as the temperature rises, the average speed of the particles increases;
- there are forces of attraction between the particles.

In the last chapter we briefly considered the nature of atoms and molecules. In order to use kinetic theory and begin to explain the behaviour of a particular material in a particular situation, we do not need to know whether we have atoms or molecules present. We simply refer to particles. We now have to imagine that these particles are not static but moving about randomly in three dimensions and at varying speeds. In any one material sample there will be millions of particles all moving differently. From our basic understanding of atomic structure, we already know that some atoms, like hydrogen atoms, are much lighter than others, such as those of lead. This is because different atoms have different numbers of protons in them. Whether the particles we are considering when using our kinetic model are atoms or molecules, it follows that those in different materials will have different masses. If you have met kinetic theory before, you will probably remember that the particles move faster as the temperature rises. What is important is that not all particles are moving at the same speed at a particular temperature. So if you have a glass of water at about room temperature of 21°C, then all the water particles will be moving around but some will be moving faster than others and some slower. If you were able to measure these speeds (you can't) and count the total number of particles, you could calculate the average speed. By heating the water, this average speed will increase. The final basic idea of kinetic theory is that something holds the particles together and prevents them from drifting apart. This means that there is always a tension between the particles moving and separating and the forces holding them together.

## Solids

Solids have a fixed shape and are difficult to compress because of the way the particles are arranged and the amount of energy they have. The amount of energy available limits the amount of particle movement; low amounts of energy mean small movements and large amounts of energy mean faster, bigger movements. For any particular material, its solid form is at a lower temperature than its liquid or gas form and the solid has less energy. This does not mean that all solids are colder than all liquids. Some materials exist as liquids or gases at room temperature and this is related to the individual particles and how they are bonded together. Oxygen is a gas at room temperature but can exist as a liquid if it is cooled.

In a solid, these low energy levels and the forces of attraction between the particles mean that the individual particles are packed closely together in orderly three-dimensional rows and their movement is restricted to a vibration. The individual particles are fixed in position within the solid. Cutting up the solid into smaller pieces means that there are more surfaces exposed and so any changes, such as melting and dissolving, will take place more quickly.

## Liquids

In a liquid, the higher energy levels enable some of the particles to temporarily overcome the forces of attraction and to move slightly further away from other particles. The particles in a liquid are more disordered than in a solid, but there may still be groups of particles showing local order. The higher energy level means that some particles move to different positions within the liquid.

A simple analogy to help you visualise the difference between particles in a solid and those in a liquid is to imagine a class of 25 pupils. It is difficult to get children to be perfectly still, so they easily represent tiny moving particles. If they are to represent a solid, you need them to form up in five rows of five standing close together. We cannot get them to stand on each other's heads, so our model is necessarily two-dimensional. If you were to push against one of the rows there would be nowhere for the pupil to go, and so this arrangement explains why solids are not easily compressed and also shows why solids have a fixed shape. There are also a lot of particles in a small space and so solids are dense materials. For the pupils to represent a liquid, they need to be given a space representing the liquid's container, and also to be told that they do not have to stand still. They are likely to move around, possibly forming small groups or areas of local order as they meet and chat to their friends, but then individuals may move on to another group. Some individuals may not move very much at all, while others represent higher than average energy particles and move about a great deal. From this model, the ability of liquids to flow and take up the shape of a container becomes apparent.

There is still not much space between the particles in liquids and so they are also difficult to compress and relatively dense. For any particular material, the solid form is denser than the liquid form, with the notable exception of water. Water particles have some unusual properties, one of which results in the solid form of water, ice, being less dense than the liquid form. This particle model also helps us to understand why some liquids are thicker, or more viscous, and others are runnier. In some liquids, the particles are still fairly close together and in others they are more spaced out. How do you think the viscosity of a liquid changes with temperature?

## Gases

The particles in a gas are very disordered and there are very large spaces between the particles. Gas particles have a lot of energy and so they are moving about so rapidly that they are much less affected by the forces of attraction that exist between individual particles. The individual particles move in straight lines until they bump into another particle, either of the same gas or a particle in the side of the container. When this happens, the particles set off in another direction, rather like snooker balls colliding against another ball or the side of the snooker table. Using our pupil model, this is like letting the children go at the end of the day!

The large spaces between the particles make gases easy to compress and the particle movement enables them to fill whatever container they are put into. The spaces between the particles are empty and so gases have large volumes and small masses, which gives them a low density. Gases float above solids and liquids; we take for granted that the air is above the land and the sea. Some gases consist of heavier particles and so are denser than others. Carbon dioxide is denser than the other gases in air and so sinks in air, a very useful property when used in fire extinguishers. The carbon dioxide acts like a blanket over the fire, preventing oxygen getting to it and so stopping the fire from burning.

Kinetic theory gives us a model that enables us to visualise and explain what is happening to the particles in a material when reversible changes occur. These are discussed later in this chapter.

## Changing state

All materials can exist in different states. Most change reversibly from solid to liquid and from liquid to gas, but a few change directly from solid to gas. Solid, liquid and gas are states of matter. When thinking about a change of state, it is important to remember that the particles do not change. We are all familiar with ice melting to form water and this evaporating to form water vapour (often inaccurately referred to as steam, which is actually condensed water vapour, that is liquid water). Ice, liquid water and water vapour are all chemically identical molecules, made up of hydrogen and oxygen atoms; they are different forms of the same chemical substance. When a change of state occurs, no new materials are made. These changes of state happen because the particles of a material either gain or lose energy. Remember that the energy level determines the average speed of the moving particles. If you heat something up, the particles have more energy and the average speed increases. Conversely, when you cool something down, the average speed of the particles falls.

## Melting

**Melting** is a change from a solid state to a liquid state. It happens when the particles in a solid begin to move around with more energy. The vibration of the particles in a solid does not disrupt the structure and the particles are held in place by the forces of attraction between them. As the energy levels increase, the vibrations become bigger and, eventually, those particles with higher than average speed are able to overcome the forces of attraction and break away from the rest of the solid structure and take on the liquid form. As heating continues, more and more particles develop enough energy to break away from the solid and take on the liquid form. Each time a particle moving at faster than average speed 'escapes' and becomes liquid, the average energy level of the remaining solid drops. This is why we need to continue to heat until the entire solid has melted but there is no change in the melting point temperature. Ice melts at 0°C and even if you put ice in a saucepan and heat it, you should record this temperature until all the ice has melted. You need to stir the ice and water as it melts and use pure water to record this value. Impure materials are mixtures and melt over a range of temperatures because each material in the mixture has its own melting point. Sometimes the source of the heating is not clear. An ice cream melts as we try to eat it on a summer's day. The ice cream is taking heat from the air that is warmer than the ice cream. If we hold an ice cube in our hand, the ice cube takes heat from our body and consequently we feel colder.

## Solidifying

The change from a liquid to a solid is called **solidifying**. It happens when a liquid loses energy and cools. The particles move more slowly and the slowest particles begin to be held in place by the attractive forces. As cooling continues, more particles will slow down and gradually the material sets and becomes solid. The point at which water becomes ice is its freezing point. The changes from solid to liquid and liquid to solid are reversible and depend on whether heat is added or removed from the material. The interchangeability of ice and water are familiar, but other common examples are melting metals in order to pour them into casts to make objects, melting solder so that it sets and secures a joint, and cooling or freezing liquids to make ice cream and sorbet.

## Evaporation and boiling

The same principles apply when liquids change to gas and when gases becomes liquids. **Evaporation** and **boiling** are changes from liquid to gas, and **condensation** is the change from gas to liquid. As liquid particles are heated, they have more energy and the fastest of them are able to escape from the attraction of the other particles and become free-moving gas particles. The particles that escape are the fastest ones, and so the average speed of the particles in the liquid falls until it is heated more. When gases cool, the slower particles are more influenced by the attraction between particles and begin to form clumps of particles, which can be seen as drops of liquid.

Evaporation means changing from liquid to gas. Liquids can evaporate at all temperatures. If you leave a saucer of water on the windowsill, the water seems to disappear. What actually happens is that the water takes heat from the air and some of the faster particles continue to move through the water surface and escape from the liquid. Evaporation takes place more quickly at higher temperatures because more particles will have enough energy to escape. A larger exposed surface area also increases the chance of particles escaping. Wet clothes dry more quickly if spread out and faster still if placed somewhere warm.

Boiling is when all of the liquid reaches a particular temperature and so many of the particles have enough energy to change state that there is a rapid change of liquid to gas. This means that bubbles of gas form and, because they are less dense than the liquid, they rise up through the liquid. If you watch water boil, the bubbles appear at the bottom of the container, near the heat source. These are bubbles of water vapour forming rapidly. Continuing to heat the water enables more bubbles to form from the fastest particles and as these escape, so more heat is needed to keep the water at boiling point. When water boils, the temperature of the water remains at 100°C until all the water has evaporated. Heating the steam will result in it becoming hotter. Different liquids have different boiling points. Alcohol boils at 80°C and this enables alcohol to be separated from water by **distillation**. By taking heat from the air, perfume in pot pourri evaporates and by using body heat, aftershave and perfume evaporate from our bodies.

## Dissolving

When materials dissolve they form a solution, which is a clear but not necessarily colourless liquid. The solid material is called the **solute** and the liquid is called the **solvent**. Many solids dissolve in water and so this is a familiar solvent, but other solvents include dry-cleaning fluid and alcohol. When a solution forms, the solid seems to disappear. We know it is still there because if it is coloured it forms a coloured solution, and sometimes it is safe to taste it – if salt, sugar or coffee has been dissolved, for example. Apart from seeming to disappear, other interesting things happen when materials dissolve. For example, if you weigh some water and begin to add some salt, the mass increases depending on how much salt is added. So if starting with 50 cm³ of water, which weighs 50 g, adding 1 g of salt produces a solution weighing 51 g. Adding another gram of salt produces 52 g of solution, and so on. If at the same time you record the volume, then the total volume does not change – there will still be 50 cm³ of solution. Even more surprising is what happens when you add 50 cm³ of pure alcohol to the same volume of water. You end up with only 98 cm³ of solution. Our understanding of particles can help us understand these results and gives us a simple model of dissolving.

## Dissolving and the kinetic theory

In a solid, the particles are arranged in close fitting rows, held together by the attractive forces. In a liquid, the particles are moving about, flowing and have a little more energy. When a solid is dissolved in a liquid, some of the liquid particles will bump into the particles on the surface of the solid and dislodge them. These solid particles are then held in the spaces between the liquid particles. Gradually, more and more particles will be brought into solution in this way. If you break up the solid into smaller pieces, there will be more surface particles to be bumped into and so the solid will dissolve more quickly. If the liquid is heated, the liquid particles have more energy and move about more and bump into the solid more frequently; hence solids will dissolve faster in hot solvents. This model of solid particles being held in the spaces between liquid particles explains why the mass increases; the solid particles are in the solution and all particles have their own mass. It also explains the volume observations; if the solid particles go into spaces, the volume will not increase. In the case of two liquids mixing, then each liquid has spaces between its particles and so they can fit between each other. A simple model of this would be mixing equal volumes of peas and sand. Stirring also increases the rate of dissolving because it increases the rate at which solid particles come into contact with the liquid particles. From this model, it also follows that there will be a point at which all the spaces have been filled, when we would have what is called a saturated solution since no more solid will dissolve in it.

## Insolubility

Some particles are too big to be held between the liquid particles and very quickly settle, even after being stirred. These substances are insoluble. Some particles are small enough to be temporarily held in the liquid, but do eventually settle. Such materials form suspensions, which differ from solutions because they are cloudy rather than clear. A good example is mixing flour and water. Filtering will separate out insoluble solids and those that form suspensions, but will not separate dissolved solids. These may be retrieved by evaporating off the water, so leaving the solid behind as a residue.

## Diffusion, expansion and pressure

**Diffusion** is a natural phenomenon by which particles spread out. This is most noticeable with smelly particles. If you spray air freshener or perfume at one end of a room, the smell can be detected at the other side of the room after a few minutes. Smoke and bad smells spread in the same way. Diffusion does not only happen in gases. If you introduce a small amount of coloured ink or food colouring into a glass of water and do not stir, it will gradually spread to give an even colour in the water. We can use our particle model to explain this. If gas particles are constantly moving, they will bump into the smell particles and set them moving in different directions. By these random collisions the smell will gradually spread. Some particles will be knocked back to where they started from but with random movement in all directions, the net result is that the smell particles will be widely spread.

With gas particles moving in all directions, some particles will inevitably bump into the sides of the container. The more gas particles in the container, the more often these collisions will happen. It is these collisions that produce pressure, and our model enables us to predict that if we increase the volume of gas in a container, then the pressure will increase and if we increase the temperature, the pressure will increase. In the first instance, because there are more particles; in the second case, because they are moving more rapidly, and in both cases collisions with the container walls occur more often.

We can use our model to explain **expansion**. As we heat materials, they expand, or take up a greater volume. When particles are heated, their movement increases and this takes up more space, although the particles remain the same size. Hold your hands together and make minute clapping movements to represent the initial vibration. Now get more energy and therefore more excited and vibrate more and begin to clap normally. The total volume occupied by your hands has increased.

## The water cycle

Water is a very important constituent of living things and so we are dependent on its supply. Ninety-seven per cent of the Earth's water is in the oceans, which leaves only three per cent as fresh water. We need fresh, not salty, water to drink and so the huge reservoir of salt water in the Earth's oceans is not directly available to us. Water is continously cycled through living organisms and the rest of the environment. This cycle depends on evaporation, condensation and precipitation. Precipitation is water falling from the air as rain, snow, sleet or hail. Some falls directly into the ocean and some falls over land, percolating through the ground into rivers and eventually into the ocean. Evaporation from the oceans, land, lakes and rivers occurs as the sun warms up the earth, and water taken up by plants also evaporates in a process called transpiration. The moisture-laden air near the Earth's surface is gradually warmed and rises, and then begins to cool. Some of the cooled water vapour condenses on small particles of dust or soot present in the atmosphere and, depending on the temperature, clouds containing water droplets or ice are formed. Surprisingly, not all clouds produce rain. The water droplets need to reach a certain size before they begin to fall and, even then, small falling droplets may evaporate again before they reach the ground. Larger drops, able to fall as rain or snow, form when more water condenses or droplets collide in the turbulent air. The cycle of evaporation, condensation and precipitation then continues.

## Common misconceptions

The idea of materials being made up of small bits is commonly accepted. What is harder to understand is that the particles are moving rather than static, and that there are always forces of attraction. When thinking about gas particles, it is commonly assumed that the forces have disappeared. The idea of space or nothingness between particles is an important part of the model that is less accepted when thinking about solids. It seems to contradict our ideas of solids being impenetrable.

When considering liquids, the particles are thought to be in a halfway state between solids and gases as regards their spacing. In reality, the particles in a liquid are much nearer to the arrangement of particles in a solid. If a model of particles in a liquid being more widely spaced is held, then it does not follow that liquids would have a fixed volume, and liquids would be compressible.

When considering the gas particle model, the empty spaces between the particles are more readily accepted, but imagining the particles as small balls results in the idea that they will all sink to the bottom of a container rather than move randomly in all directions.

In considering change of state, the fixed nature of the particles is ignored and the particles are thought to expand rather than move faster. When thinking about solutions and particles, there is a tendency to refer to the solid particles as being dispersed while ignoring the presence of the water particles.

One of the main problems with understanding the kinetic theory is that people tend to remember the diagrams that they have seen in school textbooks and, while they are able to reproduce them, they do not apply the model when asked to explain phenomena.

### Review Questions

1  What are the four basic ideas of the kinetic theory?

2  Why do solids have a fixed shape, which is difficult to compress? Why do liquids flow?

3  Why are some gases denser than others?

4  What happens when materials change state?

5  Explain the difference between evaporation and boiling.

6  Why does your cup of tea cool faster if poured into a shallow wide cup rather than a tall thin mug?

7  Why does the mass change, but the volume stay the same, when you add salt to water?

## Review Activities

1   Look up diagrams showing particles in solids, liquids and gases. Do they show the liquid state accurately?

2   Measure the temperature of ice and then freeze some salty water and measure the temperature. Research and explain why the sea does not freeze as easily as freshwater lakes.

3   Use the particle model to make your own diagrams to illustrate dissolving (remember both the solute and solvent), diffusion (remember the air particles), increasing gas pressure as the volume of the container decreases, and expansion in a solid.

4   Find out more about cloud formation.

# CHAPTER 8

# Chemical changes and basic geology

## QCA Units

This chapter supports the teaching of the following QCA units:

- Rocks and soils
- Reversible and irreversible changes

## National Curriculum

This chapter supports the following sections of the National Curriculum:

- Key stage 1 Changing materials
- Key stage 2 Changing materials

By reading and reflecting on this chapter, you should have developed your learning about materials and be able to:

- Explain the difference between reversible and irreversible changes.
- Describe and explain burning, cooking and rusting as examples of irreversible changes.
- Recognise the fire triangle and relate this to fire safety.
- Explain what happens when acids are neutralised.
- Discuss the weathering of rocks and how soil is formed.
- Know the three types of rocks and explain how they are interrelated in the rock cycle.

## Irreversible changes

Raw materials can be changed in a variety of ways. Some of these changes are easily reversible. When wet, gentle heating can dry materials. Further heating or cooling can result in a change of state, as discussed in the previous chapter. However, very strong heating, such as burning, may result in an irreversible change. Industrial and manufacturing processes change materials, making new materials for further processing or for making new objects. Making objects such as woodcarvings and wooden furniture, or processing materials such as refining salt, refining oil and spinning wool do not involve making new materials. Other processes do result in new materials being made – cheese is made from milk, pottery from clay and bread from flour. Other common examples of processes that result in new materials being made are cooking, burning, neutralisation, rusting and, on an industrial scale, making fertilisers, detergents, household cleaners, cosmetics, plastics and artificial fibres such as nylon and polyester.

## Chemical changes

A **chemical change** is a change during which new materials are formed. This is because there is a rearrangement of the atoms present. A simple model to represent this is to imagine two simple structures made from Lego bricks in which different coloured Lego bricks represent different types of atoms. Imagine a wall six bricks wide by two bricks high in yellow and a solid block made of twelve blue bricks. You can make two smaller yellow brick walls or change the blue bricks into a wall structure, but they would still be structures made of only yellow or blue bricks. Such changes represent simple reversible physical changes in which no new materials are made. Breaking the structures apart and joining yellow and blue bricks to make a two-coloured structure would represent a chemical change in which a new material is made. Applying our Lego brick model to chemical structures, then the proportion and arrangement of the atoms determines what the material is; different combinations constitute different materials. During a chemical change, it is important to note that all the individual bricks or atoms remain unchanged. None of the bricks are destroyed and no new ones spontaneously appear; we end up with the same number of bricks as we started with. In chemical changes, the individual atoms are not changed but they are rearranged to form new molecules. In the same way as the total number of bricks remains the same, in a chemical reaction the total mass of the new materials formed is equal to the total mass of the original reacting materials.

Some chemical changes are reversible, but many are not easily reversed. We can observe chemical changes in our everyday lives. As new materials are formed, we may observe fizzing or bubbling when a gas is being given off, a new substance appearing in a liquid if an insoluble precipitate forms, a temperature change making the substance hotter or cooler, a red glow or even brighter flames, or we may see a colour change.

Examples of these changes are the fizzing that occurs on our tongue as sherbet is mixed with our saliva, adding liver salts or indigestion tablets to water, milk turning sour and forming a solid, lighting a candle, burning wood and igniting fireworks. There are some important chemical changes in biology; respiration and photosynthesis are fundamental processes and both involve a complex sequence of chemical reactions in which new substances are made.

## Heating and burning

When materials are heated, they may change state or dry out as they give off moisture. For example, soft wet clay dries and becomes hard but, if made wet again, will soften. If drying continues, a different change occurs and new materials are formed. Some materials, when heated, decompose or break up into simpler materials. If heated strongly, calcium carbonate, commonly known as limestone or chalk, gives off carbon dioxide and leaves calcium oxide behind. This calcium oxide, or lime, was used in early theatres to produce limelight, a strong light given off when lime burns. Many substances burn when heated and are described as **flammable**. Some of these are useful fuels and are used to give us heat and light.

When a material burns, it reacts with the oxygen in the air to produce new materials, including an **oxide**. Heating a small piece of magnesium results in it burning with a very bright flame and a white powder being formed. This white powder is magnesium oxide. If the magnesium is carefully weighed before being heated and the powder is weighed afterwards, the powder weighs more. This is because atoms of oxygen have been added to the magnesium to make a new substance, the magnesium oxide. The oxygen atoms were present in the air and if they could have been weighed before the reaction, the same total mass of materials would be present before and after burning magnesium.

## A burning candle

If mixtures or compounds are burnt, then more than one product can result. A familiar example is the burning of a candle. When we light a candle, we can see both changes of state and burning taking place. If you look carefully at the wax at the top of the candle, you will be able to see that the solid wax melts to form liquid wax. This liquid wax then evaporates to form wax vapour, and this is in the darker central part of the flame just above the wick. Some of the liquid wax may dribble down the side of the candle and as it cools, it solidifies.

As well as these changes of state, the candle is burning. When asked to explain this, most people initially think that it is the wick that burns. Some even think that the candle is just there to support the wick and the candle gets shorter as it burns because the wax evaporates. Some wax does evaporate and if you place a burning candle on a windowsill next to a cool window, you may find drops of condensed and solidified wax on the

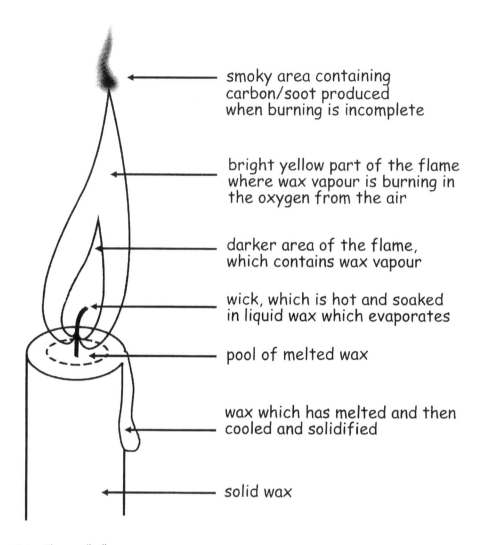

smoky area containing carbon/soot produced when burning is incomplete

bright yellow part of the flame where wax vapour is burning in the oxygen from the air

darker area of the flame, which contains wax vapour

wick, which is hot and soaked in liquid wax which evaporates

pool of melted wax

wax which has melted and then cooled and solidified

solid wax

**Figure 8.1**   The candle flame

window. However, most of the wax burns and as it burns it can be seen as the candle flame. The wick also burns, but very slowly with a red glow that can be seen if you look closely. The wax vapour burns and produces carbon dioxide and water. These are the oxides produced from the carbon and hydrogen atoms present in the candle wax. Some of the wax does not burn completely and instead of carbon dioxide being made, carbon is present in the flame. This gives a smoky flame and the carbon or soot can be detected by passing a plate over the top of the candle. To demonstrate that it is the wax vapour that burns, let the candle burn steadily for a few minutes. Meanwhile, prepare a candle snuffer and then hold a lighted match. Snuff the candle, remove the snuffer and move the lighted match towards, but not touching, the wick. If you look very carefully, you will see that the flame 'jumps' back to the wick. It is actually igniting the vapour-air mixture still present near the top of the candle.

## Cooking

When we cook, we change the materials or ingredients that we started with. In some cases, for example when cooking pasta, there are no new materials formed – the pasta simply expands and softens as it becomes wet. Other materials change because their chemical structure has been changed. This change can be detected because of a change in colour or appearance. Cooking a raw egg changes the colourless albumen to white and yolk to a different yellow. The albumen contains proteins and when these are heated, their complex three-dimensional structure is broken down. Bonds between different parts of the molecule hold the protein structure together, but heating the protein causes the atoms to vibrate so violently that these bonds are broken. The protein coagulates and sets in a new shape and the protein has been denatured.

During breadmaking, chemical reactions take place, so that new products are made. The yeast used in breadmaking is a living organism that feeds on the sugar added to the flour-and-water mix. As the yeast uses the sugar, it breaks it down into carbon dioxide and alcohol. The springy gluten molecules in the flour trap the carbon dioxide gas and so the dough rises. Using flour with less gluten in it does not make very good bread. When baked in the oven this structure sets, because the gluten molecules are proteins and they become denatured when heated. Sometimes on opening the oven, you can just detect the small amount of alcohol that has evaporated.

When cakes are baked, the carbon dioxide that produces the light texture is the result of a chemical reaction between additives in the self-raising flour. This is an example of a neutralisation reaction and will be discussed further later in the chapter. The bubbles of gas become bigger as vapour from the evaporation of water in the cake mix is added to them during cooking. The proteins in the flour are denatured when the cake is baked, and this holds the mixture of fats and carbohydrates in their new shape. In general, fats and carbohydrates are not changed chemically during cooking; it is the changes to the proteins in food that cause the observable differences. The additives in baking powder and self-raising flour react together to produce a gas to make the end product lighter and spongier.

## Rusting

Iron is a relatively common metal and has been used since ancient times to make a range of metal objects. By adding other elements such as carbon to it, a mixture called steel is formed. Changing the mixture by adding different proportions of other elements enables different types of steel to be produced. However, iron reacts with oxygen when water is present to form iron oxide or rust. Rusting is a form of metal corrosion, as the metal is gradually 'eaten away' leaving the much weaker and powdery rust. Rusting is a complex, irreversible chemical change that needs both water and oxygen to be present for the reaction to take place. Cleaning steel nails with abrasive paper, and then leaving them in a range of conditions, enables the rusting process to be investigated. Nails left in water but also exposed to the air will rust fairly quickly. Nails completely immersed in tap water also rust because the water contains dissolved air, and nails left in damp air will also rust. Nails left in completely dry air do not rust, nor do those left in water that has been boiled for a few minutes to remove the dissolved air. The nails can be treated in various ways to prevent rusting, such as covering them with grease or painting them.

## The fire triangle

Burning usually requires a heat source to get the reaction started. Not many materials will spontaneously burn when exposed to the oxygen in the air and those that do have to be treated with extreme care. Other materials will burn steadily once they have been heated initially, often by using materials that ignite more readily. We use firelighters to start our barbecues and chemicals on the end of matches to light cigarettes. For burning to take place three things are needed, heat, oxygen and the fuel. A **fuel** is any material that burns in oxygen to release the energy present in the fuel-oxygen system. For a fire to continue to burn, fuel, oxygen and heat are still needed. They form the three parts of what is known as the fire triangle. Removal of any one of these will put the fire out. This means that putting out a fire needs it to be cooled, or the fuel to be removed or some way of smothering the fire so that oxygen does not get to it. Using cold water to cool the fire is often effective but not suitable if oil is burning or it is an electrical fire. Covering flames with a heavy blanket or carbon dioxide from a fire extinguisher can smother the fire. Making a firebreak by isolating the fire from more fuel can be used in forest fires by cutting down and removing trees so that the fire then burns itself out. Using the right method is very important and it is best not to tackle a fire incorrectly but to evacuate to a safe place and leave fire fighting to the experts.

## Neutralisation

### Acids

When non-metal elements form oxides that can dissolve in water, a group of chemicals called **acids** are formed. Acids are distinguished by their properties. In foods, acids have a sour taste. Other acids may be corrosive, toxic, harmful or irritant. Acids can corrode metals, making them appear dull rather than shiny as the acid eats away at the metal. Tasting is never a good way of finding out about unknown fluids!

It is important to distinguish between the terms **concentrated** and **strong**. It is possible for acids to be concentrated and strong, or concentrated and weak, or dilute and strong, or dilute and weak. Concentrated strong acids are not safe to handle without suitable precautions, but we can handle and even eat dilute weak acids. A concentrated acid is one that has not been diluted or mixed with very much water. A strong acid is one that has very acidic properties. Concentrated, strong acids are corrosive, which means they eat away at other materials that they come into contact with. When acids react with metals, they release hydrogen gas, observed as fizzing. In the strongest acids, this fizzing is very rapid. Examples of strong acids are hydrochloric acid, nitric acid and sulphuric acid. Familiar weak acids include vinegar, with the chemical names acetic or ethanoic acid, lemon juice (which contains citric acid), vitamin C or ascorbic acid, and carbonic acid, which is formed when carbon dioxide dissolves in water. Carbonated fizzy drinks are weakly acid because carbonic acid is formed when carbon dioxide is added to the drink or the water. Other examples of common acids are cream of tartar and sour milk.

It is also possible to change the concentration of the acid. Acids are solutions in water and a concentrated acid is made with less water. Using more water results in a more dilute acid. Diluting an acid does not change it from a strong to a weak acid because there are still the same number of 'acid particles' in it; they are just more spread out.

## Alkalis

When metals form oxides that can dissolve in water, they produce **alkalis**. Alkalis are a subgroup of chemicals called **bases** – those chemicals that are the opposite of an acid and which can neutralise them. Alkalis are also distinguished by their properties. Like acids, many alkalis are also corrosive, toxic, harmful or irritant, and they may feel soapy. As with acids, alkalis can be strong or weak, concentrated or dilute. Some common alkalis are ammonia, bicarbonate of soda, toothpaste, bath salts, washing soda, washing-up detergents, cement and lime. An example of a strong alkali is sodium hydroxide. Some household cleaners, such as dishwasher detergent, are very alkaline and corrosive and need to be handled with care.

## Indicators

In chemistry, indicators are used to find out whether a solution is acidic, alkaline or **neutral** (that is, neither acidic nor alkaline). **Universal Indicator** is made from pigments which change colour depending on the strength of the acid or alkali. Very strong acids turn the indicator red and very strong alkalis turn it blue. There is a range of intermediate colours and each is given a **pH** value between 1, for the strongest acids, to 14 for the strongest alkali. A value of 7 denotes neutral and the universal indicator appears green. Other pigments also change colour depending on whether the solution is acidic or alkaline. Litmus is used in secondary school chemistry, but indicative colour changes occur with blackcurrant, beetroot and red cabbage juices. These are red in acids and blue in alkalis. If you add bicarbonate of soda to green cabbage as you cook it, it turns slightly blue, and not very appetising! Soil test kits use indicators to test the pH of soils. Different plants grow best in different types of soil. Testing your garden soil and knowing its type can save the disappointment of planting an expensive azalea or rhododendron and then finding that it does not thrive or dies because you do not have the right type of soil for it to grow well.

## Neutralisation

Acids can be neutralised by adding an alkali to them. Indigestion remedies are alkaline and are used to neutralise excess stomach acids. Toothpaste is alkaline so that it neutralises the acids formed on our teeth by the action of bacteria feeding on the sugars that are left on the teeth after eating. If left unneutralised, these acids begin to rot the teeth because the acid reacts with the calcium salts in the tooth structure. As a result of mixing an acid with an alkali, a chemical reaction takes place in which the molecules are rearranged and new substances are formed. In the neutralisation reaction, water and a chemical salt are formed. So when hydrochloric acid is mixed with sodium hydroxide, the salt formed is sodium chloride. When nitric acid is mixed with sodium hydroxide, the salt formed is sodium nitrate. In both cases, the salt dissolves in the water formed during the reaction and so, without using an indicator, it is difficult to detect that anything is happening. Adding a suitable indicator allows us to see a colour change as the acid is neutralised.

Acids can be used to produce carbon dioxide gas. As mentioned earlier, self-raising flour contains additives that react when the flour is wet. About two per cent of self-raising flour is made up of bicarbonate of soda, an alkali, and an acid. When moistened these react together and the bicarbonate is broken down and releases carbon dioxide. Adding acids to bicarbonates results in fizzing as the gas is given off. Try adding vinegar or lemon juice to bicarbonate of soda. In general, adding an acid to a carbonate results in the gas carbon dioxide being given off, with water and a salt being left. When vinegar, which is acetic acid, is added to bicarbonate of soda, carbon dioxide, water and the salt sodium acetate is formed. 'Alka-Seltzer' is made from citric acid and bicarbonate of soda and, when added to water, will fizz as the carbon dioxide is released. Our stomachs produce hydrochloric acid as part of the digestive process, but sometimes we produce the acid when there is no food to digest or we produce too much acid. This can lead to heartburn or indigestion. Indigestion remedies contain alkalis which act to neutralise the acid in the stomach. They are made from a weak alkali; a strong one would also be corrosive and be painful.

## Weathering and soil formation

Rock is the material of which the Earth is made. It is made up of minerals, which are elements and compounds. There are different types of rocks and these have different properties, such as hardness. All rocks, even hard ones, are subject to weathering. This is the process by which the rock is broken down into smaller pieces by the action of the weather; wind, water, temperature changes and the action of chemicals. Weathering results in the formation of soil. The topsoil is made up of sand, formed from rocks such as granite, and clay, formed from rocks such as basalt, mixed with humus, formed from decayed plants and animals. Larger pieces of rock remain as stones.

Freeze-thaw is the process by which water breaks down rocks. Water penetrates into tiny cracks and holes in the rock. When this water freezes, it expands and pushes against the rock, so opening the crack or making new cracks. These larger spaces are penetrated by more water and so the process continues. Some rocks are more porous than others and thus even more susceptible to this process.

As the Earth's temperature changes daily, becoming hotter during the day and colder at night, so rocks are heated and cooled. Hot rocks expand and cool rocks contract. The different minerals within the rock will expand and contract by different amounts and this sets up stresses in the rock, which result in it cracking and breaking. The cracks facilitate further weathering by the freeze-thaw process.

The wind carries fine grains of sand and these act like sandpaper, rubbing against larger rocks. Over very long periods of time, this constant rubbing has an effect. The surface is worn away and more fine grains are carried in the wind. We have all felt this abrasion when there is a sudden gust of wind on a beach.

Chemical weathering occurs when the minerals in the rock react with acids in rain to form new materials. Sometimes this causes the rock to change colour. We can observe colour changes in new buildings which are not due to soot or other deposits. This 'mellowing' may be due to chemical changes taking place as the rock is exposed to other chemicals in the air. Buildings and statues made of limestone are susceptible to being eaten away by acids in the rain – both the strong acids formed from the oxides of nitrogen and sulphur released when fossil fuels are burnt, and the weaker acid formed as carbon dioxide dissolves in water.

## The movement of rocks and the rock cycle

Rocks are both eroded, or worn away, and transported to new locations by the action of water, wind and glaciers. The wind is able to carry smaller pieces of weathered rock. Strong winds can carry larger grains, sometimes long distances. Lighter winds carry the smaller grains. Sand from the Sahara sometimes reaches southern England, leaving a powdery deposit. Glaciers are frozen rivers that flow slowly. As they flow, they scrape the land surface below them and any rocks carried in the glacier increases this abrasive effect. They also push rocks out of their path and carry other rocks in the glacier over long distances, depositing them as the ice around the rock melts. The water in rivers acts in a similar way. At their source, rivers flow quickly and so larger rocks can be carried in the river's current. The flow of water over the land surface gradually erodes it so that the river forms a bed that gradually deepens over time. As a river nears the sea, it flows more slowly and carries smaller particles, such as silt and clay, which are often deposited in river estuaries. This deposition of sediments can build up to form new land. This new land may be susceptible to flooding, but is also rich in minerals and is therefore very fertile. These areas are called deltas.

There are three main types of rock and they are able to change from one type to another over millions of years in a sequence known as the rock cycle. Weathering, transportation and deposition are important parts of this cycle, but there are other processes involved as well.

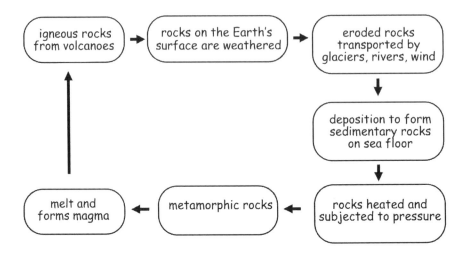

**Figure 8.2**   The rock cycle

**Magma** is molten rock found below the Earth's crust. The Earth is made up of four layers. On the outside is the thin crust, which lies on top of the rocky mantle, which extends half way to the centre of the Earth. Underneath the mantle is the liquid part of the iron core, and at the centre of the Earth is the solid core. You can picture these layers by imagining a scotch egg. The crust is the layer of breadcrumbs on the outside, the mantle is the sausage meat, and the two parts of the core are the white and yolk of the egg. The Earth's crust is thicker where the continents are and much thinner under the oceans. It ranges from about eight to about 20 kilometres deep. The mantle is about 3,000 kilometres deep and the core roughly the same.

## Igneous rock

The thinner, weak areas of the crust represent areas of volcanic activity, and periodically the liquid material of the mantle escapes to the Earth's surface as lava. These eruptions may lead to the formation of volcanoes as the lava builds up near the point of eruption. The rock that reaches the Earth's surface is called **igneous rock**. After eruption, the lava begins to cool and minerals in the molten rock begin to solidify and form crystals. The rate of cooling varies. When igneous rock cools quickly, small crystals are formed, while slower cooling produces large crystals. Basalt is a rock in which the lava cools exposed on the Earth's surface and so relatively quickly forms small crystals, whereas granite has large crystals because it remains under other layers and cools more slowly. These crystals are seen as sparkles in the rock and make granite paving stones and kerbstones look attractive. Another difference between basalt and granite is that the minerals that make them up are different. Basalt has basic (alkaline) properties and reacts with acids, and when weathered the grains contain complex silicates that give rise to silt and clay which produce good soils for plants to grow. Granite weathers to leave silicon oxide grains or quartz, recognisable as sand grains. Loam soils give good fertility and drainage because they contain both sand and clay.

## Sedimentary rock

As these igneous rocks are weathered, they are transported and then deposited. These deposits build up at the bottom of the sea over very long periods of time to form **sedimentary rocks**. As the sediments form, other things, such as dead plants and animals, may also fall to the bottom of the sea and so become part of the sediment and may give rise to fossils. As the layers in the sediment build up, the lower layers become compacted because the pressure on them increases while, at the same time, trapped water is pushed out. This causes the rock grains to stick together and form sedimentary rock. Good examples of sedimentary rocks are limestone and chalk, which are built up from the shells of sea animals; mudstone, which is formed from mud, and sandstone from sand grains. Sedimentary rocks are layered and the oldest layers are at the bottom. Once dated, these layers provide reference dates for any fossils found within them.

## Metamorphic rock

Sedimentary rocks can undergo further changes. As they become buried deeper in the Earth, so they begin to heat up. The action of heat and pressure on the minerals in the rock causes new crystals to form. This recrystallisation process gives rise to the third type of rock, **metamorphic rock**. Limestone is changed into marble, and slate is formed from shale. Any fossils present in the original sedimentary rock will still be present in the metamorphic rock. Metamorphic rocks are hard and their crystals are often arranged in layers. This explains why slate is relatively easily cut into thin pieces used for making roof tiles.

## Common misconceptions

If the nature of elements and compounds is not understood, then the concept of new materials being made, rather than a material changing its state, is not clear. The distinction between the changes associated with a liquid evaporating is not perceived as different from burning to produce gases in the air. The involvement of invisible components, such as gases, in a chemical reaction tends to be ignored. This is true whether the gas is a reactant or a product. By ignoring these components, the conservation of mass is difficult to appreciate, and this leads to the idea that when things burn, they become lighter because material is burnt away.

The categorisation of reactions into reversible and irreversible is more readily understood than a distinction between chemical and physical change. However, using irreversible for chemical changes is incorrect, and many chemical changes are reversible. A better understanding of chemical change depends on an understanding at the particle level.

An understanding of acids and alkalis develops from an everyday understanding about acids – for example, as met in crime stories in which they are used to dispose of bodies or to produce horrific injuries with burnt flesh, the corrosive properties of battery acids, and the effect of acid rain on buildings and possibly plants. It is generally thought that acids are dangerous, and so appreciating the difference between strong and weak, concentrated and dilute is important.

When studying rocks, the word *rock* can initially be interpreted as a large jagged lump rather than a general term for the material making up the Earth's crust. Rocks tend to be thought of as being made of only one type of material, and so granite is not appreciated as a mixture. The difference between natural and artificial causes confusion; rocks are perceived as natural, and so polishing or treating them – for example, in making marble worktops – leads to the idea that the material is no longer natural. The material is, but the object is not. Although the process of sedimentation is understood it is more difficult to link this to sedimentary rocks, which are often still perceived as volcanic. Understanding weathering depends on an appreciation of the timescales involved and the freeze-thaw cycle requires knowledge of the forces produced as water freezes and expands.

## Review Questions

1  How would you distinguish between a reversible and an irreversible change?

2  What do you mean by a new substance being made?

3  Explain how a candle burns. What changes are taking place?

4  What sort of change is involved in baking bread and cakes? How do you know what type of change is involved?

5  Distinguish between concentrated and strong acids. Give examples of strong and weak acids.

6  Give examples of the use of the neutralisation of acids.

7  Explain weathering and its role in the formation of sedimentary rocks.

## Review Activities

1 Try out the Lego model of changes. Starting with two or three different colours in blocks, how many new materials can you make?

2 Carefully watch a candle burning and try to relight it from a distance, as suggested in the text.

3 When cooking, look at the colour and texture changes that take place.

4 Try adding blackcurrant juice to lemon juice, colourless vinegar, lemonade, baking powder and toothpaste, and observe what happens.

5 Try to collect samples of igneous, sedimentary and metamorphic rocks.

6 Look for signs of weathering on limestone and sandstone buildings, and note the use made of different rocks, such as slate on roofs and granite and marble used as decorative facing.

# CHAPTER 9

# Forces in key stage 1

## QCA Units

This chapter supports the teaching of the following QCA units:

- Pushes and pulls
- Forces and movement

## National Curriculum

This chapter supports the following sections of the National Curriculum:

- Key stage 1 Forces and motion
- Key stage 2 Forces and motion

By reading and reflecting on this chapter, you should have developed your learning about materials and be able to:

- Describe the effects that forces have on objects.
- Interpret diagrams showing forces acting on objects.
- Explain the difference between speed and acceleration and how forces are involved.
- Define inertia and momentum.
- Explain why some objects float and others sink.
- Discuss the forces affecting objects that are moving horizontally.

## Forces and their effects

Simply, forces are pushes and pulls. We can feel pushes and pulls with our own bodies – for example, when we try to slide or drag heavy objects along a floor. We readily associate force with our hands or feet touching the object we are trying to move. Other objects exert forces on each other, but we may still be able to observe contact between objects – for example, when snooker balls or marbles collide, and we can see the result of this force because one ball has pushed the other and affected its movement. We are also familiar with some invisible forces, such as magnetism, because we can still see their effects. Sometimes, as in the case of the magnetic force, we use the words *attract* and *repel* instead of *push* and *pull*. Electrostatic attraction, observed when we rub balloons and stick them to walls, is another example of an attraction or pulling force. There are other pushes and pulls that we meet so often in our everyday lives that we tend to forget they are there. Friction and gravity are particularly good examples.

Forces have effects on objects that we can observe. They can:

- start things moving;
- stop things moving;
- speed things up;
- slow things down;
- change the direction of movement;
- change the shape of the object.

We can experience all of these for ourselves using balls. Place a ball on a flat surface and give it a little push; it starts moving. Push it again in the same direction and it moves faster. Keep doing this and it soon gets too fast to keep up with! Pull or push the moving ball in the opposite direction and it slows down and can be made to stop. Push a moving ball from the side and it changes direction. Pressing down on the top of a ball can squash it and change its shape.

## Representing forces in diagrams

When describing forces, we need to know the direction of the push or pull; the effect is different depending on the direction. We also need to know its size, or magnitude. A bigger force will have a bigger effect. In diagrams, forces can be represented by arrows that show the place where the force is acting on the object, the direction of the force and the size of the force by using a scale in which the length of the arrow represents the magnitude of the force.

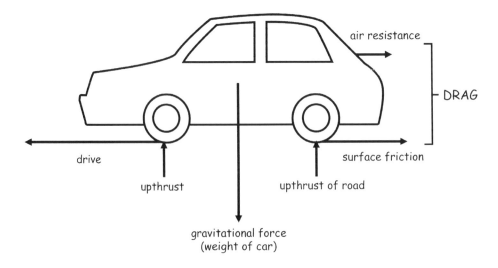

If drive exceeds drag, the car moves forwards and accelerates.
If drive equals drag, the car moves at a steady speed.

**Figure 9.1**   Diagrammatic representation of forces

### Speed and acceleration

**Speed** is a measure of how fast something is moving. We are familiar with miles per hour, in which we state how many miles we will travel in one hour. In science, we use metres per second or centimetres per second. This can be written as m s$^{-1}$ or cm s$^{-1}$. Speed is calculated by dividing the distance travelled by the time taken. Knowing how fast an object is moving is useful information but it is often just as important to know what direction it is moving in; whether a car is speeding towards us or away from us affects our decision about moving out of the way! To describe an object's movement in terms of its speed *and* its direction, we use **velocity**.

**Acceleration** is defined as the change of speed that occurs over a period of time. If an object gets faster, it is said to accelerate; and when it slows down, it decelerates. Deceleration is given a negative value to indicate that the speed is decreasing rather than increasing. So 3 metres per second per second means the object is speeding up but minus 3 metres per second per second means it is slowing down. To calculate this, you measure the speed of a moving object twice and know the time interval between measurements. Using a speed gun, you could measure the speed of a car in metres per second as it crosses a line on the road and measure it again 30 seconds later. Calculate the difference between these two speeds divided by 30. The units are metres per second, per second. This is the increase or decrease in speed in metres per second that takes place each second.

When studying moving objects, there are some important points to note. The first is that all moving objects would continue to move if no force were acting on them. We always expect objects to stop moving and so this idea, Newton's First Law of Motion, is very counter-intuitive. Our understanding of the movement of objects has been developed while living on Earth, where there are always forces affecting the objects around us. One is gravity, which makes things fall towards the centre of the Earth, and another is friction. It is difficult to imagine a situation in which these two forces are not having an effect, but it is by imagining these conditions that we are able to predict and explain how objects will move in a variety of situations. To explain an object's movement, it is important to know whether it is moving at a steady speed or accelerating. From our initial statement of the effects of forces, we can see that once an object is moving at steady speed, it does not need to have a force acting on it, but an object accelerating or decelerating does. There may be more than one force acting on an object. When forces are acting and the result is a steady speed, then the forces are balanced. If the result is acceleration, then the forces are unbalanced and one of the forces is having a greater effect. It is particularly important to realise that it is forces that bring about actions and that acceleration is the *result* of forces acting. It is not true that the acceleration *causes* the force or that it *is* the force. When a car accelerates, it is the drive from the engine that provides the pushing force. A bigger engine can produce more drive and more acceleration!

To summarise, when trying to explain an object's behaviour in terms of forces, we need to know if it is moving or not and, if it is moving, whether it is moving at a steady speed or accelerating. A stationary object either has no forces acting on it (difficult to achieve on Earth) or the forces acting on it are balanced. The explanation for an object moving at a steady speed is the same as for a stationary object. An accelerating object has unbalanced forces acting on it.

## Moving things, inertia and momentum

If you are in a car when the brakes are suddenly applied, you don't slow down but continue to move forward, until stopped by your seatbelt. Although we know that on Earth objects eventually do slow down and do not keep on moving forever, we also recognise that not all objects in the same conditions slow down at the same rate. We need to use more force to stop a heavy, fully loaded supermarket trolley than an empty one. Similarly, if we have two cardboard boxes of the same size and fill one with books and the other with soft toys, we know which one will be easier to get moving along a wooden floor. This reluctance of an object to accelerate or decelerate is called **inertia**. Heavier objects have more inertia, and inertia is directly related to the amount of 'stuff' or matter in an object. We measure the amount of 'stuff' in an object, its **mass**, by using scales and recording the result in grams or kilograms. Inertia is a property of an object that is directly proportional to its mass.

Another word commonly used when talking about moving objects is **momentum**. Forces are needed to slow things down, and the amount of force needed depends on the momentum the object has. The ability to slow down an object is not only related to its mass or inertia. The amount of acceleration or deceleration is also important. As has been explained above, a bigger force is needed the heavier an object is, and if two objects have the same mass, more force is needed to slow down the object that is moving faster. Something moving faster needs more deceleration in order to stop. This means that the force needed to stop an object moving is equal to its acceleration multiplied by its mass, and this is its momentum. All forces are measured in units called **Newtons** and this relationship between force, mass and acceleration is used to define the value of one Newton. One Newton is the force needed to accelerate one kilogram at a rate of one metre per second per second. We use this relationship without thinking when we kick or throw a ball, although some people are better at making judgements than others and so become, for example, star footballers or netball players.

## Floating and density

### Density

**Density** is relative heaviness. If we have two objects of the same volume and we compare their heaviness, we are actually comparing their density. Imagine comparing a full litre carton of orange juice with an empty one. Of course, we could just put the cartons on a balance and the full one would give a bigger mass reading. The important thing to note about density is that it also takes into account the volume of the object. We cannot always have objects of exactly the same volume and so density can be calculated by dividing the mass by the volume. Relative density is a measure of how the density of substances compare with water. The mass of one cubic centimetre of water is one gram, and so water has a density of one gram per cubic centimetre. From our understanding of solutions and a model of the solute particles being held between the water particles, it can be predicted that a salt solution would have a bigger density than water because its mass per cubic centimetre would be bigger. The more concentrated the solution, the greater the density. In general, because solids have their particles more closely packed than the liquid state of the same material, the solid is denser than the liquid. Water and ice are notable exceptions. This is because when ice forms, the solid particles are actually more separated than they are in water, where the attractive forces between the water molecules act to make water more compact.

When materials of different densities are mixed together, those that are denser will sink and those that are less dense float. Air floats on water; hence when a bottle or jar is pushed below the surface of water, bubbles of air can be seen rising up through the water. We are so used to air being above water or land that we don't think about it. Similarly, we expect the land to be underneath water or air and stones to sink if we throw them into the sea or a pond. Oil is less dense than water and so we can see spilt oil floating on water, while on wet roads small amounts of oil can give puddles an iridescent appearance. Different materials have different densities. In general, gases are less dense than liquids and liquids are less dense than solids. However, there are dense liquids, mercury for example, and solids such as balsa wood that are less dense than water. Comparing materials and objects and their densities relative to water is easy.

Using a collection of solid and liquid materials and a range of objects, we can find out whether they sink or float when placed on water. Add oil to water and it floats, but add golden syrup and it sinks. Less dense materials float on water and those that are denser sink. Gases are less dense than water but they also vary in their density. Carbon dioxide is a good example of a gas that sinks in air, which is why it is used in fire fighting and to give a theatrical drifting smoke effect.

## Floating objects

So why do boats, which are made from the dense material steel, float? We can make any material float by creating an object with a large volume, so that when the overall density is calculated it is less than that of water. Often, when creating the object, we make space in it that becomes filled with air, which is much less dense than water and so reduces the overall object density. Another way to make an object float is to place it in a denser liquid, such as very salty water. Remember that we can easily float in the Dead Sea!

When an object is put into water, it displaces or pushes some water out of the way. If you completely fill a container, such as a mixing bowl, and add the object, you can catch this displaced water by placing the mixing bowl in a larger washing up bowl. The amount of displaced water is equal to the volume within the water taken up by the object. If the mass of this displaced water is more than the mass of the object, the object floats. If it is less, the object sinks.

## Upthrust

We can explain why things float in terms of the forces acting on the object. If we drop an object such as a ball into water, we will initially see it moving downwards. For an object to start moving, a force has to be acting on it, in this case gravity. When the ball stops moving downwards, then another force has stopped it. This is true whether it has come to rest at the bottom of our container or if it is floating on the surface; something has stopped the movement. The name for this force is upthrust. We can use our understanding of particles to help us imagine this. All materials are made up of particles that are moving and attracted to each other. When the ball pushes against the water particles, it will tend to push them further apart, while the attraction between the water particles tends to hold them together. If the push from the ball is stronger, the water particles separate and the ball sinks. If it is weaker, then the water particles push back and the ball floats. This pushing back of the water particles is upthrust. If resting on the bottom of the solid container, the particles of the container are much more closely packed and so a much greater push is needed to separate them. A very heavy ball could crack the container!

We can continue to use this model to consider streamlining. A streamlined shape can push through the water particles much more easily and so will sink to the bottom of the water more quickly. Having a blunt or flat end to the object makes it more difficult to push the water particles, because the push is over a larger area. Try pushing a knife through butter using the blade correctly and then on its side.

## Moving horizontally

We can start something, such as a toy car, moving horizontally by pushing or pulling it. If we want to find out more about this movement, it is helpful to be able to control the conditions so that what happens in different situations can be explained. We may want to know the effect of changing the surface, of an oil or water spillage, or of pushing harder. There may be some things we could change that have no effect. By trying things out, we can begin to build a picture of how moving objects behave. Our prior experience may tell us that pushing an object across an ice rink or air hockey table feels different from pushing it over a polished floor or carpet. In order to recognise small differences, it is helpful to take some measurements. If we push an object, such as a toy car, over various surfaces, it is relatively easy to measure or mark how far it travels before it stops. To be able to make meaningful comparisons, we would need to be sure that the object was pushed with the same amount of force each time and that we did not change the object, but only the surface it is moving across.

## Making fair comparisons

One simple way of doing this is to place the toy car at the top of a ramp and let it go. The toy car rolls down the ramp because the force of gravity is pulling it downwards. As the car moves, this force is still pulling on the car and so the car moves faster. The car accelerates down the ramp. As previously explained, the amount of acceleration depends on the amount of force, in this case gravity, which remains constant. As long as we start the car at the same height up the ramp when we let go, each time the car will be accelerated down the ramp by the same amount. Any differences we notice in the distance the car travels from the bottom of the ramp will be caused by the different surfaces. Remember that in order for an object to stop moving, a force needs to be acting. In this situation, the car stops because of friction, and different surfaces generate different amounts of friction as the car travels over them. There is friction between the car and the ramp and between the moving parts of the car, but this friction is the same each time the experiment is carried out and so will not affect the results. Some cars have wheels that turn very easily, but other cars have a lot of friction as the axle turns. This means that it is not possible to compare different surfaces using different cars. The friction between the car and the ramp and that associated with the axle is the reason why it is possible to place a car on a ramp and for it not to start moving. Friction holds stationary things in place and does not only occur when objects are moving. If we increase the height of the ramp, the car will have longer to accelerate and will have been pulled down the ramp by gravity for longer, so we are using a bigger force. This means that we can compare how far a car travels when pulled by different amounts.

A different way of changing the amount of force is to use a simple catapult made from elastic bands. If you interlink three or four bands and then stretch them between the legs of a chair, you can use this simple catapult to start objects moving. The further the elastic is stretched the greater the pushing force. This technique works well with old margarine tubs weighted down with plasticine, so that they travel along the floor. Different surfaces, such as different types of sandpaper, can be stuck to the bottom of the tub in order for comparisons to be made.

## Friction

**Friction** is a force that gives us grip. This holds stationary objects still and stops or slows down moving objects. It is the interaction between the two touching surfaces that produces friction. The more these two surfaces are in contact, the greater the friction. This means that if we push down on the toy car as it moves along, there is more friction, because we are pushing the surface of the tyres into closer contact with the floor. This will be more noticeable on carpet than on a wooden floor, because we can push further into the carpet. **Gravity** pulls things downwards and so making the car heavier has the same effect as pushing down on it. The relationship between increasing the mass of the car and the amount of friction can be calculated mathematically, but note that it is not true that doubling the mass, doubles the friction. As stated earlier in this chapter, the inertia is doubled, and so it is more difficult to get a heavier object to start moving but, once it is moving, the increase in friction is not as great. If we are trying to slide a heavy box or supermarket trolley along the ground, it is difficult to start it moving and we need to push hard, but once it is moving, It Is much easier and less pushing force is needed to overcome the friction.

Both of the surfaces contribute to the amount of friction. Two coarse surfaces produce a lot of friction and two very smooth surfaces produce very little. If you imagine the coarse surface as a series of jagged bumps, then as the surfaces rub across one another, the bumps interlink and fit between each other and need to be pushed over each other. A smooth surface does not impede movement in this way. If you have one smooth and one rough surface, sometimes there seems to be only a little friction. This is because the area of contact between the surfaces is very small because only the tops of the bumps rub across the smooth surface. There is more friction when there is more surface area in contact. That is why ice skates have narrow blades; it reduces the contact between the skater and the smooth ice. There needs to be some friction to stop the skater falling over! The tyres on racing cars provide another interesting example. Smooth racing tyres have a larger surface area than grooved tyres and so produce more friction, and yet this enables the cars to go faster. This apparent contradiction is because the tyres also provide grip, and the drive from the powerful engine needs to be able to push against the road in order to move forward. If you follow Formula 1 racing, you will have heard a lot of talk about the amount of down force the cars need in order to be able to be controlled and steered round corners. In the wet, the road surface becomes very smooth because of the lubricating effect of the water, and this drastically reduces the friction between the tyre and the road surface. In these conditions, grooved tyres work best because the grooves push the water away from the road surface, so that the tyre is in better contact with the road. The grooves reduce the amount of tyre surface in contact and so the cars are not able to travel as fast, but they can be steered! The same is true of our own cars – bald tyres would not be a problem to us in perfect driving conditions, but any water on the road and we would go out of control. We are unlikely to stop and change our tyres if it rains, so for safety it is important to have suitable grooved tyres.

Friction slows down moving objects and also acts to provide stability. Although perhaps annoying when we are trying to push something or move quickly, it is a very useful force and we would find it very difficult to live without it. When we join things together with nails, screws or glue, we are relying on friction to hold things in place. Friction allows us to stand and sit without sliding, to construct buildings and control movement. More about friction as things move through the air is in the next chapter.

## Common misconceptions

Forces present many problems in understanding because we have learnt to live in the world with moving objects about which we need to make predictions – for example, deciding if it is safe to cross the road, timing our catching of a ball and pushing the supermarket trolley so that it moves at a comfortable speed. All this experience means that we have ideas that are in conflict with the view given by physics. These misconceptions include the idea that a moving object has a force within it; it has been given the force when it was pushed or pulled. This leads on to the idea that the object will stop moving when the force is used up. This also links to the idea that a stationary object has no force. Having read this chapter, you should recognise that the ideas provided by physics allow us to explain movement in a range of conditions and that this explanation takes into account those forces, such as friction and gravity, that simpler everyday explanations have ignored.

Other common misconceptions are that movement means that a force is doing something and that continued movement requires a continuing force. In fact, if a force is continually acting, acceleration results and if it stops acting, there will be constant speed unless another force causes movement to slow or stop. This requires us to understand the difference between constant speed and acceleration and to realise that an increase in speed is not the same as an increase in acceleration.

Also, when thinking about forces, there is a tendency to assume that there is force acting in the same direction of the object's movement, but forces can combine their effects, thus resulting in movement in a different direction. Snooker teaches us that hitting or pushing against a ball in one direction can make it travel at an angle. In physics, all objects are seen to follow the same rules, but in everyday thinking there is a tendency to categorise things into stationary objects, those that move of their own accord (balls, for example) and, thirdly, those things that are being actively pushed or pulled, such as the supermarket trolley. Friction is not thought of as a force but as something that is associated with rubbing and heat production. This may be because forces are more readily associated with getting things going than with slowing or stopping them.

## Review Questions

1  List the effects forces have on objects.

2  Distinguish between speed, velocity and acceleration. How could you make a ball accelerate across the floor?

3  What is the difference between inertia and momentum?

4  Explain why a ball of plasticine will float if it has polystyrene in the middle, but not if it is solid plasticine.

5  Describe the forces affecting a toy car from the time it is released at the top of a ramp until it stops moving.

6  What differences would you expect if the car was:

   a) bigger and heavier?

   b) fitted with smooth tyres?

   c) running on carpet rather than wood?

## Review Activities

1  Push and pull a ball to get it to start and stop moving, move in a different direction, accelerate and decelerate, and squash it to change its shape.

2  Try to float a range of materials and objects. What shape are objects that float? What materials sink?

3  Using a large lemonade bottle filled with water, drop small differently shaped pieces of plasticine into it. Find the most streamlined shaped by measuring which sinks to the bottom quickest.

4  Repeat your sinking, floating and streamlining experiments with concentrated salt solution or oil instead of water.

5  Make a ramp and observe the effect on a toy car placed at the top of the ramp. Try ramps of different heights. Are there any heights at which the car does not move? Does it move faster with a higher ramp? Is it accelerating or moving at a constant speed?

# CHAPTER 10

# Forces in key stage 2

## QCA Units

This chapter supports the teaching of the following QCA units:

- Magnets and springs
- Friction
- Forces in action

## National Curriculum

This chapter supports the following sections of the National Curriculum:

- Key stage 1 Forces and motion
- Key stage 2 Forces and motion

By reading and reflecting on this chapter, you should have developed your learning about materials and be able to:

- Explain the difference between a magnet and magnetic material, and describe some magnetic effects.
- Select and use the most appropriate forcemeter to measure forces and understand the relationship between load and extension.
- Distinguish between mass and weight and have developed your understanding of gravitational force.

- Discuss the effects of friction in air and water in terms of air resistance and water resistance.
- Use the terms free fall and terminal velocity correctly.

## Magnets and magnetic materials

Magnets are familiar and fascinating objects. We immediately notice their ability to stick together and to a selected range of other objects. Less immediately apparent is the ability of magnets to repel other magnets. This sticking together is referred to as attraction and is an example of pulling force. When magnets repel it is an example of a push. Magnets are materials that have the ability to attract and repel other magnets over an area called the **magnetic field**. This field exists in three dimensions and its effect gets weaker further away from the ends of the magnet. The end of the magnet is called the **pole** and all magnets have two poles. These poles are known as the north-seeking pole and the south-seeking pole. Suspending the magnet in the Earth's magnetic field and observing which end points to or seeks the geographic North pole identifies them.

Permanent magnets do not readily lose their magnetism and are made from iron, nickel or cobalt. Steel is a mixture that contains iron and is also used to make permanent magnets. These magnets are identified by their ability to repel other magnets. Magnetic materials can become magnetised when near or touching another magnet. Such materials are attracted to both ends of the magnet and are never repelled. This ability to repel is the essential difference between a magnet and a magnetic material. A common misconception is that all metals are magnetic, whereas they need to contain iron, steel, nickel or cobalt.

### Magnetic poles

A bar magnet clearly has two ends, one is the north-seeking pole and the other is the south-seeking pole. These terms are often abbreviated to north and south, but this can lead to confusion about why the north pole of a magnet is attracted to the Earth's North pole. The Earth can be imagined as containing a giant bar magnet with its south pole pointing to the Earth's geographic North, and this giant magnet has a magnetic field extending around the Earth. When two magnets are brought together, the magnetic fields interact and like poles repel and unlike poles attract. So if a magnet is free to move in the Earth's magnetic field, the north pole of the bar magnet is attracted to the south pole of the Earth's giant internal bar magnet. In other words, the bar magnet points north-south and the end pointing north is labelled N.

Spreading magnetic materials, such as iron filings or small plotting compasses, around a magnet and observing how they are orientated shows the area of magnetic force around a magnet. This allows the extent and direction of the field to be shown. For a bar magnet, the field is strongest at the poles and the field lines are plotted showing the direction the north-seeking end of a compass would point, which is towards the magnet's south pole and away from its north pole.

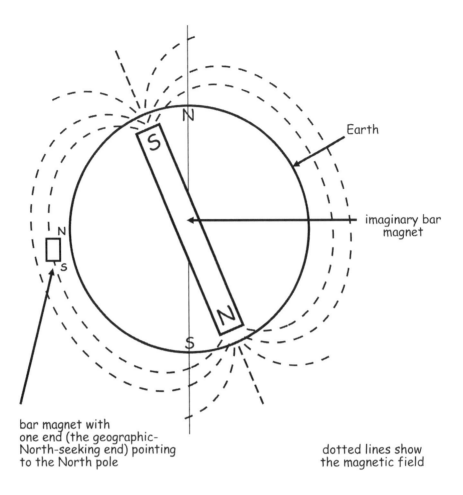

Figure 10.1   The Earth's magnetic field

## Magnetic fields

Magnetic fields extend through other materials. Magnets attract magnets and magnetic materials through water, glass, wood, paper and plastic, for example. This means that if you drop something magnetic into water, you can retrieve it using a magnet. You can also move magnetic things on a table surface by having a magnet underneath the table, or move ball bearings inside a plastic container without taking the lid off. Try finding out what thickness of paper is needed before the magnet is no longer able to cause a small magnetic object to move across the surface of the paper. The further from the magnet, the weaker the magnetic field, so by increasing the thickness of the paper, you are testing the extent of the magnetic field. Some magnets have strong magnetic fields and some are weaker. Weak magnetic fields attract over a shorter distance.

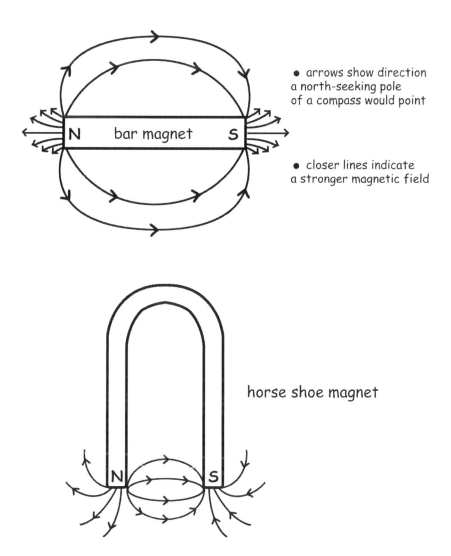

- arrows show direction a north-seeking pole of a compass would point

- closer lines indicate a stronger magnetic field

horse shoe magnet

**Figure 10.2** Magnetic fields

## Theory of magnetism

A simple way of picturing a magnet is to think about what would happen if you were to cut the magnet in half. Each half would be a magnet. By breaking a magnet up into smaller and smaller pieces, you end up with lots of small magnets. So if you imagine lots of areas within the magnet, each capable of being a tiny magnet, then if they are all lined up with their north poles in the same direction, you would have a strong magnet. This is why you can make a magnet from a nail by stroking it in one direction with a magnet. You can also demagnetise it by hammering, heating or dropping the magnet as all the tiny magnets become randomly arranged. Magnets also gradually become demagnetised over time as the tiny magnetic poles at the ends repel each other. Using pieces of iron as keepers across the ends of pairs of magnets stops the magnets losing their magnetism, because the iron becomes magnetised and so there is always a north pole attracting a south pole.

When a magnetic material is placed in a strong magnetic field, all the 'tiny magnets' line up and the magnetic material is an induced magnet. Once moved out of the magnetic field, the magnetism is lost as these tiny magnets become randomly arranged. Paper clips readily become induced magnets when brought near to a bar magnet, and chains of them can be held as each magnetised paper clip attracts the next.

The link between electricity and magnetism is amazing and useful. A current flowing in a wire has a magnetic field, and this field can be used to produce a magnet. By placing an iron core in a coil of wire, a very strong magnet is produced when the current is turned on. These electromagnets are very useful and found in electric motors, loudspeakers and telephones. A moving magnet inside a coil of wire generates current, and this is the basis of dynamos and electricity generation.

## Forces and their measurement

### Elastic bands and springs

In Chapter 6 there is a description of elasticity. Materials that are elastic are able to stretch and return to their original size when no longer being stretched. Up to a point known as the elastic limit, the amount of stretch depends on the amount of force. As the amount of force is doubled, the amount of stretch is doubled. This is not a doubling of the overall length but of the increase in length, known as the extension. So if you start with an elastic band that is ten centimetres long and pull it so that it is 11 centimetres long, you would need to pull twice as hard to make it twelve centimetres long. When you stop pulling, the elastic band returns to its original length of ten centimetres. If you keep pulling the band, it may break or become permanently stretched. Once the band has been stretched too far, it no longer obeys our doubling rule, as it has passed its elastic limit. Springs behave in the same way. Springs can also be pushed or compressed but still follow the same rule; more compression with more pushing force.

### Units of force

This simple relationship provides a mechanism for measuring forces. The unit of force is the **Newton**, named after Sir Isaac Newton. Gravity causes falling objects to accelerate towards the centre of the Earth. One Newton is the amount of force needed to cause a mass of one kilogram to have an acceleration of one meter per second per second. By hanging kilogram masses onto a spring, the extension of the spring can be calibrated or marked in Newtons. Newton meters, used to measure forces in a range of situations, are simply calibrated springs. We can find out how much force is needed to open a door or drawer, how much force is needed to stop a car rolling down a ramp or to hold an object suspended in mid-air. The object needs holding up because gravity is pulling it down, and so in this situation we are measuring its **weight**. Weight is always measured in Newtons and is due to the effect of gravity. On Earth, the effect of gravity is constant and so there is a simple relationship between mass and weight, so much so that in everyday language we use the term weight even when measuring in grams or kilograms. Technically, we should call this *mass* because it relates to the amount of 'stuff' or matter present. This mass would not change if we were to take the object somewhere where there is no gravity. However, the pull of gravity on the object would become zero in these circumstances and so the object would have no weight; it would be weightless.

We use the relationship between mass and weight to make balances, and so the situation is potentially very confusing. It is important to remember which units to use. If you want to know how much 'stuff' you have, you need to use kilograms and grams. If you need to know how much force is being used, you need to use Newtons. If you need to think about the forces in a situation where an object is being pulled down by gravity, you need to remember that this measurement in Newtons is the weight of the object.

## Gravity and weight

Referring to gravity as gravitational force can help to clarify our thinking. By reminding us that it is a force, it prompts the questions of whether it is a push or a pull, which direction it acts in and what its magnitude is. Gravitational force is a pull towards the centre of an object such as the Earth. It is not an adhesive or sticking force and does not act like a piece of elastic attaching us to the Earth; such a force would get stronger the further from the Earth that you go. As you go further from the Earth, the effect of gravity becomes less, but it does not stop having an effect once you pass beyond the atmosphere! All objects, including people, have a gravitational force, but the size of the force is related to the mass of the object. Very big masses have very large gravitational forces – for example, the Sun has about 28 times as much gravitational force as the Earth, and the gravitational force on Jupiter is over two and a half times the force we experience on the Earth. The Moon is a much smaller mass and the gravitational pull on the Moon is only one fifth of that on Earth. This makes it much easier to jump, and pictures we have seen of men on the moon show them moving very differently as they appear to float across the surface. All objects attract each other with their gravitational force, but the pull produced by relatively very small objects, such as ourselves, within the gravitational field of a much larger object, such as the Earth, is negligible. The Earth's gravitational pull keeps the Moon in orbit around the Earth, and the Moon's gravitational pull affects the water in the sea to give us our tides. At a point between the Earth and the Moon, the two gravitational forces are balanced, and at this point an object would not be pulled down to the Moon's surface or down to the Earth's surface; it would be weightless.

We recognise the effect of the pull down towards the Earth's surface as our weight. This is a measure of how much pull we are experiencing. A bigger mass is being pulled down by a bigger force. A one kilogram bag of sugar is being pulled down with a force of ten Newtons and a force of 700 Newtons is pulling down a 70 kilogram person. We all know that bigger masses have bigger weights! What is more difficult to appreciate is that the result of the bigger pull on the bigger object is the same as the effect of a smaller pull on a smaller object. Even though being pulled with a bigger force, the 70 kilogram object accelerates towards the Earth at the same rate as the one kilogram object, unless they are affected by air resistance. If there is only gravity acting, the movement of the object that is caused by gravity is called **free fall**.

## Dropping things

By experimenting and dropping objects that are not greatly affected by air resistance, we can see that when we drop objects from the same height, they all land at the same time. Try joining a few paper clips into one bunch and ten times as many into another bunch and drop them at the same time. Compare two marbles securely wrapped in clingfilm with ten or more. Drop two matching rulers, after having first added plasticine to the end of one of them, and notice that it does not make a difference. This can be difficult to believe, and you may want to increase the dropping height – because some people believe that there is a difference but that it is so small that it cannot be detected unless the fall is big enough for the difference to be measurable. There *will* be a difference if air resistance affects the object. Note the difference when you drop a piece of flat paper and one that has been crumpled into a ball.

These two observations – that all objects fall at the same rate and that gravity has a bigger pull on a heavier object – seem to be accepted when considered separately, but when they are considered together, the result is counter-intuitive and confusing. I have said that all objects fall at the same rate. In the last chapter, I said that, because gravity continues to pull on the object for the whole time it is falling, the result is acceleration. The object gets faster and faster as it falls. Once it is moving, a further pull will increase its speed because that is one of the effects of a force. So, all objects accelerate towards the ground and yet bigger objects are being pulled with a bigger force, 70 times as big in the example of the bag of sugar and a person quoted earlier. So how does a bigger force not make the object fall more quickly? The best way to imagine this is to think of the gravitational force being made up of invisible things called Newtons. Each Newton can pull on 100 grams and make it accelerate towards the ground. So, if you have 200 grams, you need two of our invisible Newtons to be able to pull the bigger object down. We accept the same relationship if we are trying to push a heavy object; we know that something twice as heavy needs to be pushed twice as hard to move as fast. The same applies to objects being pulled by gravity. A bigger mass needs a bigger force, but it will drop at the same rate.

To complicate things, we have experienced many falling objects that do not fall at the same rate. Compare dandelion or maple seeds with acorns and conkers; consider the effect of parachutes and feathers and we find the idea of objects falling at the same rate impossible to believe. These differences are because we are dropping objects through the air, and the effect of **air resistance** will be considered next.

## Friction in air and water

In Chapter 9 we discussed friction when two surfaces interact in horizontal motion. From our understanding of particles, we also know that liquids and gases are made up of particles. This means that as objects move through liquids or gases, they also rub against these particles and produce friction. In a gas such as the air, there are fewer particles to interact against a solid moving through it, and so friction is less but still has the effect of slowing things down

When an object moves through the air, we call this air resistance or drag. In water it is called water resistance. If we try to run holding an opened umbrella in front of us, we can feel this drag. Cars are now designed to reduce drag by being more streamlined. A streamlined car will travel faster with lower fuel consumption because it is the car's drive force that has to overcome drag in order to move the car forward. Boats moving across the surface of the water have a streamlined bow or pointed end, which cuts through the water. Moving vertically through water was discussed in Chapter 9 and so in this chapter, we will consider objects moving vertically through the air in more detail.

When objects fall through the air, gravity is pulling the object down and air resistance is slowing the fall. This means that air resistance is a force that acts in the opposite direction to gravity. In the air, the air particles rub against the object causing friction. The more rubbing or interaction between the air particles and the object, the greater the air resistance will be. An object falling faster will have more air resistance, and one with a large surface area will be more affected than one with a small surface area. Some objects also trap the air underneath them and this also slows them down. This effect is noticeable if you watch a sheet of paper fall. It can seem to sway from side to side as it falls. This is because as air is trapped, the paper is pushed to one side and the trapped air escapes. This side of the paper then falls more quickly and this causes the air trapped on the other side to escape, and so the swaying continues until the paper reaches the floor.

## Terminal velocity

The faster an object is falling, the more air resistance it will produce because there will be more particles rubbing against the object. So, if gravity and air resistance are affecting an object, the effect of gravity does not change, but the effect of air resistance depends on the surface area and the rate at which the object is falling. Imagine a ball being dropped. When just released, the gravitational force pulls it down and the ball will accelerate. Initially, the air resistance will be low as it is the result of the amount of surface contact and the ball's speed, which is relatively slow, because the ball has only just started moving. Once the ball has been accelerating, its speed will increase and so the amount of air resistance increases. The gravitational force does not change and, so, as the ball gets faster, there will be a time when the air resistance has increased enough to counterbalance the gravitational force, providing the ball drops from a big enough height. The air resistance acts to slow the ball down and so, when the two forces are balanced, the ball continues to fall but at a steady speed, known as the **terminal velocity**. The ball does not stop dropping, it just stops accelerating or getting faster.

Different objects reach their terminal velocity in different amounts of time. With a bigger parachute, terminal velocity is reached more quickly because the bigger parachute builds up more air resistance more quickly. A heavier parachutist reaches the ground sooner than a lighter one because, although the air resistance is the same, the gravitational force is bigger on the heavier one and so he or she accelerates for longer before reaching terminal velocity.

Trapping air in the parachute is similar to the upthrust objects experience in water. The particles are squashed together and so push back against the parachute. Eventually, some of the air is pushed out sideways and the parachute sways from side to side, similar to the way a sheet of paper sways as it falls. Putting small holes in the top of the parachute allows some of the trapped air to escape from the top of the parachute, and so the fall is more directly vertical and easier to control. If you make toy parachutes from fabric or small plastic bags, you will find that they work best with small holes in the top and small weights such as paper clips or a toy parachutist attached to the end of the strings. The weight increases the gravitational force acting on the parachute so that it falls vertically and accelerates sufficiently to build up trapped air.

## Upthrust

Upthrust in water is the force pushing up against an object, and if this balances the gravitational force pulling it down, then the object will float. A submerged object also experiences upthrust and this can be measured by attaching the object to a Newton meter. Measure its weight out of the water and then in the water. The weight in the water will be less, and the difference is the upthrust provided by the water. You can only do this with an object that would otherwise sink. If it was not attached to the Newton meter, it would sink to the bottom and the bottom of the container would provide the upthrust. Remember that if an object is not moving, there are either no forces – which is not possible, with gravity acting in this case – or the forces must be balanced. We also experience upthrust when we hold objects in our hand. Try holding a heavy book on your outstretched hand for a few minutes and then ask a colleague to take it off. Your hand will move upwards because whilst you were holding the book, you were pushing upwards to balance gravity and stop the book from falling. Once the book is removed, you can see the extent of this upthrust because it takes your body a short time to adjust to the change.

## Common misconceptions

The misconceptions associated with magnetism are that air is thought to be a requirement for a magnetic field to exist. This leads to the assumption that the Earth's magnetic field does not extend beyond the atmosphere. Magnetic poles are recognised as the ends of a bar magnet but are not thought of as the areas of strongest magnetic force. The importance of repulsion as being the way to identify magnets is not appreciated, and it is common to think of magnets only in terms of attraction. Young children think that all metals are magnetic because many common metallic objects contain iron or steel. It is therefore useful to test magnets against copper pipes and aluminium cans.

Recognising forces as occurring in pairs is difficult. The idea of a balancing force, such as upthrust, is often overlooked when thinking about forces. There is a tendency to think about only one of the forces. When an object falls or a spring is stretched, the effect of gravity is recognised, but not that of the opposing force, such as air resistance or upthrust.

Gravity is often associated with the air. When there is no air, there is no gravity is a commonly held view. This means that people think that the Earth's gravitational force stops at the edge of the atmosphere and that in space all objects are weightless. It can also result in people believing that there is no gravity on the Moon because there is no atmosphere. Conversely, other people believe that because there is less gravitational force on the Moon, there is less atmosphere but that the Moon still has an atmosphere. A view in which gravity is associated with the air can also result in the thinking that it is the air pushing the object down rather than the Earth pulling an object down. It can also lead to an idea that gravity does not act in water. This can be reinforced by thinking that floating objects are held up by the water, and not appreciating that they are also being pulled down through the water.

The change in the effect of gravitational force with distance from the Earth is not always clear. Gravity can be incorrectly thought of as being like an elastic band, so that the further from the Earth you are, the more you are pulled back. The idea of gravity being associated with all objects is difficult. Many people believe that gravity is a property of the Earth, and possibly other objects in the solar system, but they do not see it as a universal property of matter. Associating gravity with the Earth alone leads to the idea that the Earth has gravity because it is spinning or because it has a magnetic field. The scientific concept of weight is difficult. It is confused with mass and not thought of as a force related to gravity. Some people separate the ideas of gravity and weight, possibly thinking of them as two different and opposed forces in which weight is associated with objects but gravity is associated with the space around the object.

Falling is often perceived as a natural event and, therefore, an analysis in terms of forces is unnecessary. When thinking about the effect of gravity, it is sometimes only thought to be active when an object is falling. This means that gravity is ignored both before and after an object falls. When considering an object on a table, this view ignores the balanced forces of gravity and upthrust, and the object is considered stationary because no forces are acting. The idea that the acceleration due to gravity is the same for all objects even though there is a bigger pull on heavier objects is commonly misconceived. Heavier objects are perceived as falling faster and as falling with constant speed rather than accelerating. This would mean that when objects reach their terminal velocity, they have slowed down and stopped, a view often expressed when looking at diagrams of falling objects even though our common sense tells us that falling objects do not hang unmoving in mid-air!

## Review Questions

1  Why is it better to use the term north-seeking pole when labelling a magnet?
2  What is the difference between a magnet and a magnetic material?
3  Why is it possible to calibrate a spring and use it to measure forces?
4  What do you understand by the term weight?
5  Explain how and why an object reaches its terminal velocity.

## Review Activities

1  Research the shape of the magnetic fields around differently shaped magnets, such as bar magnets and horseshoe magnets, and when two magnets are in close proximity.
2  Drop a variety of objects that have different masses but low air resistance, such as paper clips and marbles, and observe them falling.
3  Drop objects that have the same mass but a different surface area, such as a sheet of paper, first dropped flat and then folded or crumpled, and observe them falling.
4  Make a model parachute and find ways of making it fall steadily by adding holes and weights.
5  Make your own forcemeter using an elastic band attached to a scale marked on card. Use different thicknesses of bands and find out what difference this makes.

# Light

## QCA Units

This chapter supports the teaching of the following QCA units:

- Light and dark
- Light and shadows
- How we see things
- Earth, Sun and Moon

## National Curriculum

This chapter supports the following sections of the National Curriculum:

- Key stage 1 Light and sound: light and dark
- Key stage 2 Light and sound: everyday effects of light and seeing
- Key stage 2 The Earth and beyond

By reading and reflecting on this chapter, you should have developed your learning about light and be able to:

- Categorise light sources as primary or secondary sources.
- Explain shadow formation for transparent, opaque and translucent objects.
- Explain why the shadow made by a vertical stick or a sundial changes during the day.

- Describe the roles of the eye and light in seeing.

- Show diagrammatically how mirrors affect light beams.

- Model the relative sizes of the Sun, Earth and Moon and how they move relative to each other.

- Use an understanding of the spin and the orbit of the Earth to explain night and day, the apparent movement of the Sun and seasonal changes.

- Recall the phases of the Moon and explain why the appearance of the Moon changes during each 28-day cycle.

## Primary and secondary light sources

Make a mental list of things that give off light. You have probably included such things as electric lights (traffic lights, table lamps, torches, fluorescent lights, etc.), candles, the Sun, the Moon, and perhaps even fireflies and glow-worms. When asked to do this, most of the things we think of are objects that actually emit light, things that are generating light. From my list, the Moon is an exception to this because it reflects the light from the Sun. A useful classification of light sources is into primary light sources, which emit light, and secondary light sources, which reflect light. Now try to think of as many secondary light sources as you can. Did you think of reflective strips on coats and shoes that enable you to be seen at night? Reflectors on bicycles? A mirror reflecting light from a lamp? The reflected light from a shiny watch or spoon that can make light patches on walls and the ceiling or can dazzle us? All objects reflect light; **bright** ones reflect more light than **dull** ones and **shiny** objects reflect more than **matt** ones. If light was not being reflected from objects, then we would not be able to see them; we would have a 'black hole'!

Darkness is the absence of light. It is surprisingly difficult to experience darkness; going deep underground and turning the lights off is a rare experience. Light is all around us and is detected by our eyes, giving us one of our main senses, sight. It is used to give warnings, for example, in traffic lights and lighthouses, and to guide, for example, streetlights and cat's-eyes on our roads. We respond to different colours and make judgements on safety and food ripeness depending on appearance. In these ways we use both primary and secondary light sources to give us information and take for granted the nature of light. Light is part of the electromagnetic spectrum and one way in which energy is transferred from place to place. Light travels in straight lines, unless something, like a black hole, causes it to bend, and this travelling takes time. However, the speed of light travelling is so quick, at 300,000 kilometres per second, that to us it appears that when we turn on a light in a room, light reaches all of the room instantaneously. It takes light eight minutes to reach the Earth from the Sun and far longer from the more distant stars, but we rarely need to think about this time delay in our view of the universe.

## Shadow formation

If light travels and takes a finite amount of time to get from one place to another, then there should be an effect if we are able to block or stop the light. Putting some objects in the path of a light beam demonstrates this effect, and we call the area where the light does not reach a **shadow**. When light meets an object it can either pass through the object, in which case the object is described as **transparent**, or it can be blocked, in which case the object is described as **opaque**. Some objects let some, but not all, light pass through them and are described as **translucent**. If you look through a translucent object, you are not able to see clearly what is on the other side, for example when trying to look through a piece of greaseproof paper. Looking through a transparent object, such as a pane of glass, enables you to see clearly what is on the other side.

When light is blocked, the object in its path is absorbing it. All objects absorb some light, even transparent ones. We can detect this because, as a result of absorbing light, the object becomes warmer; a pane of glass is warmed as sunlight shines through it and we become warmer if we sunbathe. Some objects only absorb some colours of light and let others pass through and so create coloured shadows. As well as being absorbed, some of the light is reflected, and this will be discussed later.

A shadow is produced on a surface or a screen when there is a light source and an object between the light source and the surface or screen. Shadow formation can be fun to explore and there are many factors to be considered. As already indicated, the type of object or material being used will affect the shadow. A very opaque material will create a dark black shadow, a translucent material a paler shadow; a transparent object creates a very faint shadow in which the outline may be darker or may create a coloured shadow. The amount of ambient or background light affects the darkness of the shadow; more light creates a greater contrast between very bright light reaching a surface and the lack of light where the shadow is formed. Depending on where the surface or the screen is in relation to the object, the shadow may touch the object, such as when we make our own shadow on the pavement on a sunny day, or it may not, for example the shadow formed on the ground as an aeroplane flies overhead. We can also make shadows on a screen when we place objects in a beam of light, as seen when using an overhead projector. When we prepare overhead transparencies, we use ink to block light and create shadows on the screen, often in the form of letters and words.

It can be interesting to explore whether shadows are the right way up or upside down. When we look at our own shadow on the pavement, it looks the right way up, but how would it look to someone else standing in front of us? Not all shadows have sharp edges. This depends on whether we are creating a shadow using a very fine beam of light which is all blocked by the object, or using a more extended light source, in which case a central dark area called the **umbra** is formed, surrounded by a less dark area called the **penumbra**. In this outer area, some light reaches the screen from some parts of the light source but not from other parts, as shown in Figure 11.1. The sharpness of

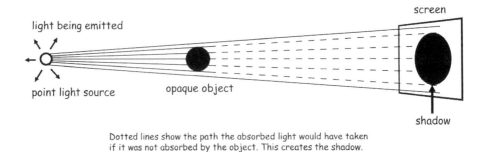

Figure 11.1   Shadows and partial shadows

a shadow is also affected by the distance between the light source and the object and by the distance between the object and the screen.

We can change the size of the shadow by changing the distance between the object and the screen. If we also use different types of objects and vary the brightness and size of the light source, we can create a range of shadow effects.

## What happens to our shadow during the day? Are we our own sundial?

On sunny days we can see our own shadow on the pavement. At different times of the day it will be a different size, much smaller at midday and longer in the evening. If we returned to the exact same spot at different times during the day and always faced in the same direction, we would also notice that, as well as changing size, our shadow would be pointing in a different direction. If we replaced ourselves with a stick or pole, we could mark the position and size of the shadow every hour and by labelling these, we would have produced a very simple sundial.

As the Earth spins, the Sun appears at different heights above the horizon during the day. When low on the horizon at the beginning and end of the day, the Sun casts a very long shadow. Try holding a pencil vertically on a table and hold a torch horizontally just above the table surface and shine a beam of light at the pencil. The shadow will be very long and on the side furthest from the torch. By moving the torch in an arc over the pencil while keeping it the same distance from the pencil, you can observe the changes to the shadows formed. When the torch is vertically above the pencil, there is a very small circular shadow.

The way in which the Sun appears to move across the sky during the day varies depending on where you are on the Earth and on the time of year. At the equator, the Sun is seen to follow a steep arc, being vertically overhead at midday, whereas nearer the North Pole it follows a much shallower arc and is not vertically overhead at midday but further south. The relative position of the Sun in the sky also changes during the year, appearing to follow a shallower arc in the winter and being further south in the winter when viewed from Britain. This means that we cannot create a perfectly accurate sundial by marking the shadows and times on one day. When used a month later, the shadows will be in a slightly different place and of a different length. However, such a homemade sundial enables us to tell the approximate time on a sunny day.

## Seeing

When light reaches an object, it can be absorbed, or it can pass through the object or it can be reflected. Secondary light sources reflect light that has been emitted by a primary light source. If this reflected light reaches our eyes, we are able to see the object that is reflecting it. Light enters our eyes through the pupil and when it reaches the retina it can cause the light-sensitive cells to respond and send a nerve impulse to the brain. The brain interprets the pattern of impulses and we see things. The eye is sensitive to the amount of light; more light will stimulate more cells in the retina. We are also sensitive to colour. Cells in the retina, called cone cells, respond to different wavelengths or colours of light. Other cells, called rods, respond to low light levels and enable us to distinguish shapes at night and when the light is dim. Sight therefore depends on light reaching the eye and setting off the chemical reactions in these rod and cone cells that result in messages being sent to the brain.

It follows from this that we only see objects that reflect or emit light. We see a candle flame because the light emitted from the flame travels from the candle to our eye. We see the Moon because the light from the Sun is reflected by the Moon and travels to our eyes. When you look around, you can see the floor, the walls and the furniture of the room you are in because they are reflecting light. Different objects reflect different amounts of light and reflect light in different ways. Very smooth surfaces are described as shiny and reflect a lot of light. Matt surfaces absorb more and reflect less light than shiny surfaces. White and pale colours reflect more light than black or dark ones. However, it is possible to have a smooth dark surface that is shiny.

## Reflection

A good reflector, such as a mirror, does not depend on the amount of light but on its ability to reflect most of the light reaching it. White paper reflects a lot of light, but glossy black paper is shiny and produces a better **reflection**, or **image**, if you use it like a mirror. To produce the best mirror image, the surface needs to be smooth and good at reflecting light. A smooth surface reflects the light reaching it without scattering it. A light beam reaching a mirror surface is reflected back as a beam of light. One reaching a matt surface is scattered and reflected back in lots of different directions. Smooth mirrors produce good clear images because of their ability to reflect light without scattering. A simple model of this is to imagine throwing a ball against a wall. If the wall is smooth it will bounce back in a predictable way. Thrown at right angles to the wall it comes back along the same path and is easy to catch. Thrown at an angle to the wall it bounces off in the opposite direction but the angle is the same. If the wall has a very rough surface, then the ball bounces back unpredictably. Smooth mirrors like smooth walls always reflect light in this predictable way and so clear images are produced. Figure 11.2 shows how light is reflected by a mirror and so to the eye appears to be coming from a spot behind the mirror, the image.

## Earth, Sun and Moon

We are very familiar with pictures of the Earth as seen from space and so readily accept that it is a sphere that exists in space. The size of the Earth is more difficult to grasp. From our position on its surface, it is huge, but then travelling to the other side of the world no longer seems such a huge undertaking; it can even be considered as a holiday destination by some. We have the ability to communicate, in what is virtually real time and in both words and pictures, with people in distant places and this can make the Earth seem quite a small place. So how big is it and how does its size compare with other familiar objects, such as the Sun and the Moon?

The Earth has a mass of $6 \times 10^{27}$ g and a diameter of $13 \times 10^3$ km. Such large figures rarely have real meaning for us, so it is useful to have comparisons. If we consider the Earth to be our standard against which we compare other objects, then the Sun has 333,000 times the Earth's mass and a diameter that is 109 times greater. The Moon is smaller than either the Sun or the Earth. Its mass is only one sixth of the Earth's mass and it has a diameter just over one quarter that of Earth. So if we want to model the relative sizes of the Sun, Earth and Moon, we can use a large beach ball about 1,400 mm in diameter to represent the Sun and model the Earth and the Moon using plasticine. The Earth would be 13 mm in diameter and the Moon, 3.5 mm. Such a model gives a very good idea of the relative sizes, but using the same models to show the relative distances between them is difficult. The distances are so big that to show them using the same scale makes the model difficult to set up. The plasticine model Earth would need to be placed 15 km away from the model Sun and the model Moon would need to be

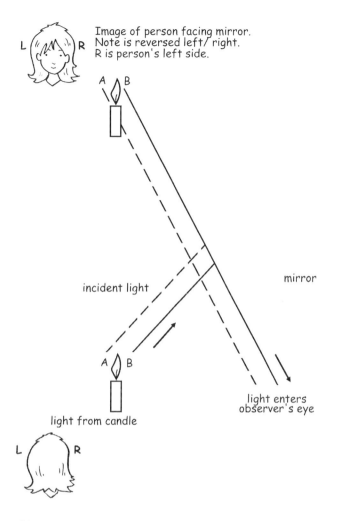

**Figure 11.2** Mirrors and images

390 mm from the Earth. The huge distances involved means that many solar system models use a different scale to represent the comparative sizes of the Sun, planets and Moon and a different scale to represent distances, often with the scale for the planets being 100 times bigger. Such a compromise enables a model to be produced in a small space, such as a school, but can mislead people into thinking that the distances between the planets are not as great as is actually the case.

The Earth moves relative to the Sun in two ways – it spins on its own axis and it travels round the Sun following a path called an **orbit**. These two movements give rise to the basic rhythms – night and day, and the year with its changing seasons. At the same time, the Moon is spinning and orbiting round the Earth as well as orbiting the Sun along the same path as the Earth. The Moon's spin and orbit of the Earth means that its appearance changes in a predictable pattern called the phases of the Moon.

**Eclipses** occur when these movements result in the three bodies being aligned. When shadows are cast by the Moon on the Earth, we experience a solar eclipse. When shadows are cast by the Earth on the Moon, we have a lunar eclipse.

## Night and day and the seasons

### Night and day

The Earth is a sphere and is opaque. This means that light reaching the Earth from the Sun does not pass through it. Some is absorbed and warms the Earth, and some is reflected, which explains why we can see the Earth from space. If you imagine having a tennis ball in a darkened room and turning on a table lamp, then you would notice that one side of the ball reflects the light and the side furthest from the lamp is dark. Mark an X on the side of the ball that is lit and spin the ball on its vertical axis. The spot marked with the X will be alternatively in the light and in the dark. This demonstrates the changes in light levels that we experience daily. During the day, we are on the side of the Earth that is facing towards the Sun, and at night we are on the side facing away from the Sun. The Earth spins on its axis once every 24 hours, producing a regular rhythm of light and dark that we call day and night.

The sun is stationary, but during the day it appears to move in the sky, getting higher in the sky until it reaches its highest point at midday, and then gradually sinking towards the horizon until sunset. To explain this, you may find it helpful to use a globe. Put a piece of blu-tack on the globe and shine a bright beam of light towards the globe. As you spin the globe, imagine that you are standing on the blu-tack. During one complete spin you will experience dark and light periods.

Using Figure 11.3, consider the view from each position A to D. At A it is midnight and the sky is dark. As the Earth spins and you reach position B, it is still night, but by looking towards the Sun, which is on the eastern horizon, you will be able to see some light. This is dawn and the Sun appears to be close to the horizon. As the Earth spins further, you will reach point C at midday, when the Sun appears directly overhead and at its highest point in the sky. At D and looking back over the western horizon the sun again appears low on the horizon and we recognise this as sunset. Now try to imagine the appearance of the Sun at intermediate points. Remember that you are close to the surface of the Earth and so cannot see very far round the Earth's curved surface. Put a cocktail stick into your blu-tack and spin the globe and you are able to model the sundial shadow changes that occur during the day.

### The seasons

The Earth spins on its axis daily and also orbits around the Sun. The orbit is a very slightly squashed circular path, an ellipse, and it takes one year to complete this journey. Contrary to popular belief, the distance of the Earth from the Sun at different times in its orbit does not significantly change. At the equator there is very little seasonal change,

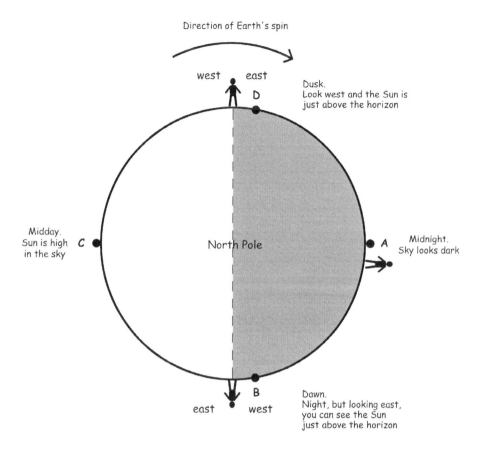

**Figure 11.3** Night and day

but in Britain we experience very distinct seasons. Seasonal change is the result of changes in the number of hours of daylight we experience at different times of the year. Long days mean that the Earth is warmed by the Sun for longer and we experience the warm weather of summer. The change in day length is caused by the tilt of the Earth. The axis on which the Earth spins does not run from the north to the south pole, but is displaced 23 degrees. During our summer, the northern hemisphere is tilted towards the Sun and countries in this hemisphere experience long days. During our winter, the northern hemisphere is tilted away from the Sun and we experience short days.

This seasonal effect is enhanced because the Earth is spherical. If you shine a powerful torch beam at the surface of a globe, you can see that the patch of light that results can be a different shape. Hold the torch at the side of the globe and shine it at the equator and you get a circular patch of light. Shine it towards Britain and you get an oval patch of light. The area covered by the light beam increases as you move away from the equator. The heating effect of the Sun is spread over a greater area, the further from the equator you are. The atmosphere also has an effect. The Sun is more directly

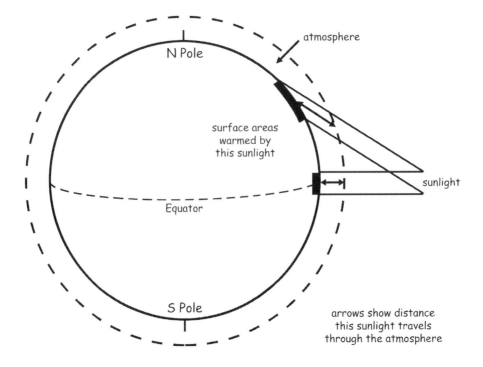

**Figure 11.4** The Sun's heating effect

overhead at the equator and so light passes through the atmosphere at right angles, whereas further north it passes at an angle and this path is longer. This results in more heat being absorbed by the atmosphere and the surface temperature being cooler.

## The phases of the Moon

The Moon can be seen from the Earth because it reflects light from the Sun. If you shine a light onto a sphere and then look at the sphere from different angles, it will look different. Look at the sphere from behind the light and it looks circular. Look from behind the sphere and towards the light and it appears as a dark area in the light. Look from the side and you will see a semi-circle or crescent shape. This shows that the changing appearance of the Moon results from a change to our viewing angle, and not because there is a shadow being cast on the Moon. The Moon orbits the Earth once every 28 days. When it is between the Sun and the Earth, we call it a new moon, and it is not visible in the sky because the light from the Sun is being reflected back towards the Sun and not towards the Earth. Very occasionally, the Moon's position is such that it casts a shadow on the Earth's surface and these events can be spectacular and are called solar eclipses. As the Moon continues its orbit, it will reach a position when it appears just before sunrise and just after sunset as a crescent shape. At this time of the lunar cycle it is common to see both the Sun and the Moon in the sky. The Moon's orbit continues and it will appear as the first quarter, or capital D shape, from noon until midnight in the west. As it continues to move around the Earth, the full moon appears in the night sky from sunset to sunrise. Finally, the Moon moves into its last quarter, or backward D shape, and can be seen in the eastern sky from midnight until noon.

Lunar eclipses occur when the Moon passes through the Earth's shadow and so does not reflect any light. This does not happen every lunar month, because it is possible for the Moon to orbit the Earth following a path that does not pass through the Earth's shadow. Eclipses occur about five times a year, two solar and two or three lunar, but most are only partial eclipses and visible from parts of the Earth that are difficult to reach. When a total solar eclipse occurs over a populated area, it is a spectacular event.

## Common misconceptions

Light beams or rays are perceived as behaving in certain ways, as observed in demonstrations using light rays, but this understanding is not related to light in everyday situations. Light sources are not always understood to be emitting light in all directions in three dimensions but rather as emitting a two-dimensional beam. Without the correct understanding, it is difficult to explain how people in different positions are all able to see the same object.

The fact that everything that we can see is either a primary or secondary light source is not appreciated. Reflection is narrowly understood in relation to mirrors or particularly good reflective surfaces. When thinking about mirrors, a common misconception is that the light stays on the mirror, making the reflection rather than being reflected and entering the eye so that the image can be seen.

Shadows are thought to only occur in bright light. Ambient or background light is not considered as affecting the type of shadow formed, and when making shadows with artificial light, there is a tendency to concentrate on the light source and ignore the effect of other light sources. Young children think of shadows as something that light reveals and so are more easily seen in bright light. Shadows are therefore seen as real objects, which are usually hidden, rather than as the absence of light.

The role of reflection in seeing is poorly understood. 'Active seeing', in which the eye has an active role, is a common idea; we see things because we are looking at them and our eyes make this possible, rather than light enabling us to see. This leads to incorrect diagrammatic representations of how we see things. Arrow lines are used to show seeing with a link from the eye to the object. Even when the role of light entering the eye from a primary source is shown correctly, a further request to show how a non-primary source is seen rarely results in the primary light source being shown, nor in the correct representation of light travelling from the primary source to the object and then to the eye.

The idea of light travelling is a difficult idea. There are misconceptions that light travels further at night, does not travel during the day, it is just there, that light is not able to travel in space or that it travels a very limited distance.

## Review Questions

1 Distinguish between primary and secondary light sources and find out more about the electromagnetic spectrum.

2 Explain how we see objects, using a diagram to represent the path of the light. Add a second observer to your diagram.

3 Explain how day length causes seasonal temperature changes. What other factors are involved in producing seasonal changes?

4 Draw a diagram to show the tilt of the Earth and its position relative to the Sun in the four seasons. Indicate the orbit direction.

5 If viewed looking down on the Earth's North Pole, which direction does the Moon take as it orbits the Earth? Draw a diagram showing the Moon's appearance at different times in its orbit.

## Review Activities

1 Try to make the 'best' shadow by varying:
   a) the type of object used, opaque or translucent or transparent;
   b) the amount of ambient light;
   c) the distances between the object, the screen and the light source;
   d) the width of the light beam from the light source.
   What does 'best 'mean? Are some shadows scarier, larger, sharper?

2 Make a simple sundial and research factors that need to be considered when making an accurate sundial.

3 Find out more about the structure of the eye and how we see peripheral movement and colour.

4 Use a mirror and a light source producing a ray of light to see how the mirror reflects the rays. Place an unlit candle in front of a small mirror and a similar lit candle behind the mirror and move it until the image appears to be a lit candle. You need to have the image positioned so that the top of the candle is at the top edge of the mirror!

5 Find out why the Moon's spin means that it is always the same surface of the Moon that faces towards the Earth.

6 Research solar and lunar eclipses.

# CHAPTER 12

# Sound

## QCA Units

This chapter supports the teaching of the following QCA units:

- Sound and hearing
- Changing sounds

## National Curriculum

This chapter supports the following sections of the National Curriculum:

- Key stage 1 Light and sound: Making and detecting sounds
- Key stage 2 Light and sound: Vibration and sound

By reading and reflecting on this chapter, you should have developed your learning about sound and be able to:

- Relate sound production to vibrations and know that a range of different sounds can be produced.
- Explain how sound travels in different materials.
- Distinguish between pitch and loudness and correctly use terms such as wavelength, frequency, amplitude and timbre.
- Describe the role of the ear in hearing.

## Different sounds

Sound, like light, is a mechanism by which energy is transferred. All sound originates with a **vibration**, a rapid to and fro movement. Depending on what is vibrating and how it is vibrating, different sounds can be produced. There are three main ways of producing sound and these are used in different types of musical instruments. Hitting an object produces percussion sounds and involves a vibrating surface, such as a drumskin, a bell or a solid object such as a table or a stone. Plucking or strumming or bowing is used with string or wire to cause it to vibrate. Good examples are the strings of the harp, guitar or violin, and a similar effect occurs when a stretched elastic band is plucked. Thirdly, vibrations can be set up in the air in pipes or tubes. Wind instruments, such as the organ, flute and clarinet, use this sound source. We can often feel these vibrations even when we cannot see them directly and it can be fun to place small pieces of paper or dry rice on a vibrating object and watch the effect! Hold an inflated balloon close to your mouth and speak and you can feel the vibrations.

Varying the tension and/or the length of the string can change the note produced. A tighter string produces a higher note. Similarly, a more stretched elastic band produces a higher note. Try this for yourself! A shorter string also produces a higher note. Varying the length of the column of air that is vibrating in wind instruments changes the note in the same way. A shorter column of air gives a higher note. You can try this by blowing across the top of glass bottles containing different amounts of water. When the bottle has only a small amount of water in the bottom a lower note is produced than when the bottle is half full of water, because the column of air is longer. Interestingly, the opposite effect is heard if the bottle is struck on the outside. The fuller bottle produces a lower note because the bottle is now acting as a percussion instrument.

The same note sounds different when played on different musical instruments. This difference in quality is called **timbre**. When a vibration is set up in a musical instrument, it is not a pure single vibration. There are other weaker vibrations and the number and strength of these overtones affects the quality of the note produced. Tuning forks are able to produce a pure sound because the vibration of the tuning fork lacks these overtones.

## Sound travels

Sound travels. We can hear sounds from some distance away, such as people talking on the other side of a room, aeroplanes passing overhead and the approach of other cars on a busy road. Unlike light, sound needs a medium to travel through. This means that sound cannot travel in a vacuum and so does not travel across space. So we do not hear any noise that the Sun might be making although we can see the Sun. This is a significant difference between sound and light.

Sound travels because of the action of the particles that make up all materials. The source of the sound is a vibration and this movement pushes rhythmically against the particles around it. So a vibrating violin string pushes against the air particles, a bell struck under water pushes against the water particles, and when we bang on a metal pipe, we push against the metal particles in the pipe. Sound travels by alternate compression and decompression, or rarefaction, of the particles in whatever is transmitting the sound. Using a slinky spring provides a good model of this. Quickly moving one end to and fro sets up a wave of to-and-fro movements that pass along the spring. It is important to remember that sound travels out from its source in all directions at the same time – rather like ripples on a pond, only in three dimensions. This means that the energy of the original vibration is spread out over an increasing volume of space and so sounds are always louder, or have more energy, the closer to the source we are.

The particles in a solid are closer together than the particles in a liquid, which are closer than those in a gas, as explained in Chapter 7. The closer the particles, the easier and quicker it is for them to bump into each other and pass the vibration along. This means that sound travels fastest in solids and slowest in gases. The speed of sound in air is 330 metres per second; it is five times faster in water, at 1500 metres per second. Sounds travel at different speeds in different solids, for example 5000 metres per second through steel and 3700 metres per second through brick. Even this is much slower than the speed of light, which travels at 300 million metres per second, and this explains why we hear the thunder some time after seeing the lightning during a thunderstorm.

**Echoes** occur when sound is reflected off a surface. This can be demonstrated with a slinky spring by placing a solid surface at the end of the spring and seeing the vibration travel back along the spring. Sound echoes are the basis for **sonar**; since the speed of sound is known, then recording the time taken for the sound to return from an object enables the distance to that object to be calculated. In some situations, it is important to reduce echoes, and so material is used which absorbs the sound. Look out for this in lecture theatres, concert halls, cinemas and theatres.

All surfaces reflect and absorb sounds. Some reflect more and others absorb more. When sound travels from one medium to another, much of the sound is reflected. This is the reason why closing the classroom door keeps the noise in the classroom, even though the sound could travel faster through the wood of the door compared with the air in the classroom.

## Sound qualities

### Pitch and loudness

Notes have two characteristics; they have different **pitch** and varying degrees of **loudness**. The pitch of a note, whether it is a high note or a low note, depends on the **frequency** of the vibration. This is how rapid the movement is. An object that is vibrating rapidly makes a high-pitched note. If you could watch the vibration and then represent it as a diagram, it would look like A in Figure 12.1. If it is vibrating more slowly it would look like B and be a lower note.

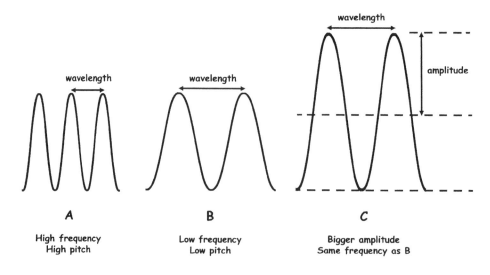

**Figure 12.1**   Sound waves: frequency and amplitude

## Frequency and wavelength

The frequency is how many to-and-fro movements there are per second and is measured in **hertz** (Hz). In Figure 12.1 it is represented by how many complete up-and-down lines there are over the same distance. The closer together the lines are, the higher the frequency. Lines that are closer together have a smaller **wavelength**; this is the time between each vibration reaching a certain point or, in the figure, the distance between peaks. Pitch results from the frequency and wavelength of the vibration.

## Amplitude and resonance

Another characteristic of sounds is their loudness. The original vibration is caused by a force acting on whatever is made to vibrate. If a bigger force is used, then a bigger vibration is produced, and this gives a louder sound. Hitting a drum softly does not produce the same effect as hitting it with a much bigger force. The bigger force produces a bigger vibration, which is a greater to-and-fro movement. This characteristic of sound waves is called the **amplitude** and is shown diagrammatically by C in Figure 12.1. This wave shows a bigger amplitude than B and represents a louder sound of the same pitch. It is the same pitch because it has the same frequency and wavelength as B.

   **Resonance** occurs when another object starts to vibrate with the same frequency as the original vibration. This happens because objects have a natural vibration frequency and when a sound of this frequency reaches an object, it will start to vibrate as well. Resonance is responsible for opera singers sometimes breaking wine glasses. If the note they are singing is the same as the natural resonance of a glass, the glass starts to vibrate and, with increasing amplitude, stresses build up in the glass until it breaks.

## Hearing and the ear

The ear is much more than the part of it that we can see attached to the side of our head. This external ear, or pinna, collects sound waves from the air and from certain solids, such as a tabletop. Try placing your ear next to the table and asking a friend to tap a pattern of sounds out on the under surface. You can also hear sounds under water; try it next time you go swimming. Quieter sounds can be detected by increasing the size of the collecting apparatus, as shown by bats which have large ears compared to their body size. Some animals are also able to move their pinna so that it points in the direction of the sound and this enables more sound waves to be collected. Try watching a dog's ears when it detects a distant sound.

The sound waves or vibrations in the air are channelled along a narrow passage to the eardrum. This vibrates and is attached to an arrangement of small bones, or ossicles, that magnify the sound wave and transmit this increased amplitude to the oval window. The frequency of the wave has not been changed. The oval window separates the air-filled middle ear from the fluid-filled inner ear. As the oval window vibrates, it sets up ripples in the fluid of the inner ear and these sound waves pass along the cochlea. In this spiral organ, there are nerve cells with hairs that respond differently to the different sound waves, and so the impulses sent to the brain are interpreted as pitch and loudness.

Our ears can respond both accurately and selectively to different sounds. People with a well-developed musical sense can detect a false note or a single incorrect frequency among many. We are all able to some extent to tune in to a single conversation against a background noise of other conversations or music being played. We take for granted the real-time nature of our ability to hear. There is no time lag between us saying something and being able to hear ourselves. We are able to detect sounds over a huge range of frequencies, from about 50 to 20,000 Hz when we are young and haven't damaged the delicate hairs in our cochlea by listening to too much loud music or by overusing a personal CD player. The ear is also very sensitive to loudness and can detect sounds that are a billion times louder than the quietest sound that you can detect.

The loudness of sound is measured in **decibels**, abbreviated to dB. This is a logarithmic scale in which twice the sound pressure, or power used to produce the sound, increases the sound level by three decibels. This means that an increase of one decibel represents a big increase in noise level. A measure of zero decibels is a sound that can only just be heard, the rustle of paper is about 30 dB, loud conversation is about 60 dB, a food blender is 100 dB, while a measurement of 140 dB can be painful and at 150 dB the bones in the ear can break. Nowadays, people are much more aware of the dangers of overexposure to loud sounds and it is common to see people working in a noisy environment wearing ear defenders. It is a combination of loudness and length of exposure that is important; prolonged exposure to loud music, for example, can cause both temporary and sometimes permanent deafness to develop.

## Common misconceptions

Even where it is recognised that sound production is associated with vibration, the sound produced may be associated with the properties of the material making the sound rather than with the difference in the type of vibration. Very young children think that beating a drum somehow releases the sound that is dormant and trapped within the drum. This also means that the sound is thought to originate in the space inside the drum rather than from the drumskin vibrating and setting off vibrations in the air inside and outside the drum.

Where vibrations are visible, for example when we pluck an elastic band, then the importance of the vibration as the sound source is more readily accepted, but the link is not usually made independently of teaching. When it is a vibration in the air – for example, after clapping our hands – or when it is a solid object vibrating, such as when stones are knocked together, it is not immediately apparent that anything is vibrating, and the sound is thought to be a result of the action, a spontaneous production rather than the action setting up a vibration.

The concept of sound travelling and taking longer than light to reach our senses is appreciated by reference to thunder and lightning, but this is not a conclusion children reach about thunder and lightning independently. It is accepted as a natural phenomenon until the relationship is highlighted. Sound is thought to travel in a similar way to light, needing an unobstructed path, possibly being imagined as an invisible ray. Later, the idea develops that air is needed, and so the idea of sound travelling through fluids and solids may be surprising.

Many people think of echoes as reflected sound, but this thinking is only applied to special circumstances where a clear reflection of sound is produced. The idea of all surfaces being able to reflect sound is not appreciated. The idea of sound being absorbed by acoustic panelling may be familiar, but it is often thought that only special materials are able to absorb sound, and not that these are materials that are simply better sound absorbers. The idea of sounds being reflected off the surface of the water as an explanation for why you cannot hear your friends talking at the side of a swimming pool when you are beneath the surface is not the initial explanation for many, who incorrectly think that it is because sound does not travel through the water.

The link between the type of vibration and pitch and volume is often confused. This is in part because of the use of a specialist vocabulary, and pitch not being linked to frequency and wavelength and loudness to amplitude. This leads to errors such as thinking bigger vibrations are both louder and higher pitched.

## Review Questions

1 What is the source of all sounds?

2 How can you alter the pitch of a sound made by a string or wire, a column of air, a drum?

3 In what type of material does sound travel fastest? Explain why.

4 Explain the difference between pitch and loudness.

5 Why does a sound seem quieter when you are further away from its source?

6 Explain the roles of the eardrum and the oval window in the working of the ear.

## Review Activities

1 Experiment with making sounds with a variety of instruments – stretched wires, bands and bottles – and vary the pitch and loudness.

2 Make simple telephones from tins and string. Cross the strings of two of these devices and set up a four-way conversation. Explain why this happens in terms of the vibrations passing along the strings.

3 Find out about the role of vibrations in the working of a microphone and a loudspeaker.

4 Research the sound levels in decibels of a range of everyday activities, such as an aeroplane passing overhead, a disco, a lorry engine, a car engine, a pop or classical music concert, a washing-machine spinning and your alarm clock waking you up.

5 Find out more about how our ears are damaged by exposure to noise.

# CHAPTER 13

# Electricity

## QCA Units

This chapter supports the teaching of the following QCA units:

- Using electricity
- Circuits and conductors
- Changing circuits

## National Curriculum

This chapter supports the following sections of the National Curriculum:

- Key stage 1 Electricity
- Key stage 2 Electricity: Simple circuits

By reading and reflecting on this chapter, you should have developed your learning about electricity and be able to:

- Set up and use electric circuits safely and know the difference between power and voltage.
- Explain electricity flow in simple circuits and the difference between electrical conductors and insulators.
- Draw and interpret circuit diagrams using conventional symbols for components.
- Explain why a lamp in a circuit lights in terms of current, voltage, resistance.
- Use models and analogies to explain electrical concepts.
- Describe the processes involved in electricity generation.

## Electrical safety and power

It is difficult to imagine living without electricity. Even when away from our homes and workplaces in relatively isolated places, we rely on electricity in a portable or battery form to power appliances such as watches and torches. Electricity is a hugely convenient way of powering leisure and labour-saving devices in our homes and at work. Children are taught at an early age to be careful with electrical appliances; responding to simple rules such as keeping electrical appliances away from water, not pushing things into electric sockets and keeping away from power sub-stations and overhead power lines. As we get older, we are told to use the correct fuse in plugs and in the household fuse box, and we also learn that when we go abroad we need special adaptors in order to use our hairdryers, shavers and other appliances.

As we are using electric circuits daily, it is a good idea to try to develop our understanding of them. We should, for example, know the difference between power and voltage, what current means and whether the electricity from a battery is different from the electricity from the mains supply. By investigating circuits and their components, we can begin to develop this understanding.

If you look at any household electrical appliance, you will find a label giving information about the power level or wattage and the voltage required. My hairdryer's label reads 230 volts and 1600 watts. This means that I can use my hairdryer with a 230-volt mains electricity supply. If the supply is a different level, my hairdryer will not work. This is because the mains voltage is a measure of the amount of energy available to push the electricity around the circuit. Different countries have developed electrical distribution systems based on different voltages. Appliances in those countries are then designed to work on that particular voltage. This is why we need an adaptor in order to use electrical items when we travel abroad. The adaptor changes the voltage, not just the shape of the plug.

## Voltage

The voltage produced by a power station is about 25,000 volts. This voltage is then increased to about 400,000 volts so that the electricity can be carried around the country along a network of cables or power lines that form the National Grid. At sub-stations, this very high voltage is then reduced either to the level needed for domestic use, 230 volts, or to a higher level for industrial use. All these voltage levels are dangerous because at these levels the voltage is enough to drive electricity through our body. Batteries produce smaller voltages, up to 12 volts, and these are much safer and do not give us electric shocks. Car batteries need to be treated with care because they have a heating effect that causes burns and they also contain acid, which is hazardous. So the **voltage**, measured in units called **volts**, abbreviated V, is a measure of the energy available to push the electricity around a circuit.

## Power

In electrical components, the electricity is used to enable things to happen. In my hairdryer, it is used to produce heat and drive a fan so that I can dry my hair. In a light bulb it produces light, in a motor movement results and in a loudspeaker sound is produced. The **power** is shown as the number of **watts** and this tells us the rate at which the electricity is being used. An appliance with a higher rating – for example, a 1000-watt hairdryer compared with a 500-watt hairdryer – will produce more heat and consume more electricity. It will therefore cost more to run because we pay for our electricity depending on how much we use. This use is measured in **kilowatt-hours**, which is the equivalent to using a 1000-watts (or one kilowatt) hairdryer for one hour. If a 500-watt dryer is used instead, then it can be used for two hours for the same cost. The power or ability of an appliance to use electricity and produce the effect we want is measured in watts, and also indicates the cost of using the appliance.

## Simple circuits

The voltage of mains electricity makes it dangerous to use to investigate electrical circuits, and so batteries are used as a source of electricity in schools. In secondary schools, power packs may be used. These are like the adaptors we take on foreign holidays – devices for changing the voltage, in this case, to produce low safe levels. So, if the voltage is pushing the electricity around the circuit and the wattage is telling us the rate we are consuming electricity, we need to be clearer about what electricity is.

Electricity is a flow of electrons and a way of transferring energy. So the energy stored in a battery can be transferred to a light bulb by the electrons flowing round a circuit. In order to clarify this, we need to consider what is happening in a circuit in more detail. A **circuit** is an arrangement that allows electricity to flow. As described in Chapter 6, materials are made up of atoms and within these atoms are smaller particles called electrons. In metals, these electrons form a sea or cloud and are relatively free to move. When a piece of metal or metal wire is joined to each end of a battery, the electrons will move along the wire. This is because the battery provides the voltage, or energy to push them along, and the electrons are free to move. We do not see anything happening but the wire may feel hot and the battery may not work next time we try to use it. In order to see an effect, we can put a simple component into our circuit. Adding a light bulb indicates when electricity is flowing because it lights up. Buzzers or small motors can also be used as indicators. Adding a switch allows us to control the flow of electrons. When the switch is open there is a gap in the circuit, and the current can only flow if there is a complete circuit of wires and working components for the electrons to flow along. Leaving a gap in the circuit stops the flow, as does adding other materials in which the electrons are not free to move.

## Conductors and insulators

Materials, such as metals, that allow the electrons to flow are called **electrical conductors**. Materials that do not allow electrons to flow are **electrical insulators**. A common non-metal that is a conductor is graphite, a form of carbon used in pencils. If you expose the graphite at each end of a pencil and connect it into a circuit, the circuit will work. The wood is an insulator and so the pencil models the construction of household electrical wires. Plastic and rubber are good insulators and are used to make a barrier to prevent current flowing where it is not wanted. Household wiring is made up of metal, usually copper, wires, surrounded by layers of plastic, similar to the way the graphite in a pencil is insulated by the wood.

## Static charge

Insulators are able to hold electrons and so build up charge. When two insulators are rubbed together, some electrons are rubbed off one of them and onto the other. In this way, they become charged because one of them has extra electrons. This charge usually dissipates but if very large charges build up, sparks or crackling can be produced as this discharge occurs. To prevent sparking in dangerous situations, such as when charge builds up as fuel runs along a pipe when aeroplanes are refuelled, a good conductor is attached to the fuel tank to provide a link to the ground, thus enabling continuous discharge. Build-up of charge that is not able to flow is called electrostatics, literally electricity that does not move. Electrostatics gives rise to many interesting phenomena, such as making our hair stand on end after vigorous brushing, rubbing balloons and sticking them to the wall, and rubbing a plastic rod or comb and using it to attract small pieces of paper. Large amounts of charge can be built up on metal objects that are well insulated; the Van de Graf generator is a secondary science favourite for demonstrating this.

## Simple circuits

In a simple circuit we need to have enough voltage to push the electrons around the conductors in the circuit. These conductors are either wires or components, and so it follows that within components there must be a path of conducting material for the electrons to flow along. Sometimes this path is hidden from view and we see only the surrounding layers of insulation. One component where it is relatively easy to see the pathway for the electrons is in a light bulb. If you look carefully, you should be able to see the filament, a special piece of wire that heats up and produces light when the electricity flows through the bulb. Less obvious are the points at which the filament joins the rest of the circuit. In household light bulbs, there are two points of connection – one is the bayonet and outer metal layer, which is in the form of a screw thread in screw type bulbs, and the other is the metal area on the bottom of the bulb, which is surrounded by black plastic insulation. The circuit therefore consists of the bottom metal connection, the filament and the outer metal connection.

## Current

When the electrons flow along the wire they do not disappear or get used up. They simply move in one direction. This flow of electrons is called the **current**. The rate at which the electrons flow is measured in **amperes** or **amps**, abbreviated as A. There is a link between the rate at which the electrons flow and the voltage or energy with which they are pushed. A bigger voltage will produce a bigger current if the rest of the circuit remains unaltered. If the electrons remain in the circuit and do not get consumed, what is it that we pay for? We pay for the energy. Very simply, as the electrons flow, they carry energy and this energy is transferred from the electrons to their surroundings very slightly as they flow along the wire and at a greater rate as the electrons flow through other components such as light bulbs. Energy transfer will be discussed in the next chapter. In the wire there is a very small heating effect, and in the light bulb there is a much greater heating effect that also produces light. It is not the electrons or current that is used up by the circuit, but the energy in the battery. The battery runs down and has to be recharged or replaced. If using mains electricity we need to pay for the energy consumed, as indicated earlier. Components vary in the rate at which they transfer energy and this is indicated by the wattage. Energy-efficient components are able to transfer more energy to produce the effect we want. This means that energy-efficient light bulbs produce the same amount of light as conventional light bulbs but with a smaller wattage.

## Circuit diagrams

When we put together a simple circuit to find out if a bulb is working or whether a material will conduct electricity, we may want to communicate our activities to others. It is helpful to have a diagram showing the circuit we set up, but drawing real components and showing them as they are actually laid out in front of us can be an artistic challenge. And it may not enable others to readily identify the important aspects of the circuit. Initially, we may want to arrange our circuit so that all the components are spread out and the linking wires clear. When circuits get more complex, this becomes more difficult as wires tend to cross one another and overlap. Circuit diagrams aid communication because they simplify and arrange the information on the page in a way that enables the circuit to be understood.

There are conventions used in drawing circuit diagrams and the components are represented by symbols. Common symbols are shown in Figure 13.1. Technically, if you are making a circuit with batteries, these are individually called **cells** and a group of them is called a **battery**, but in everyday language we refer to individual cells as batteries, as I have in this text.

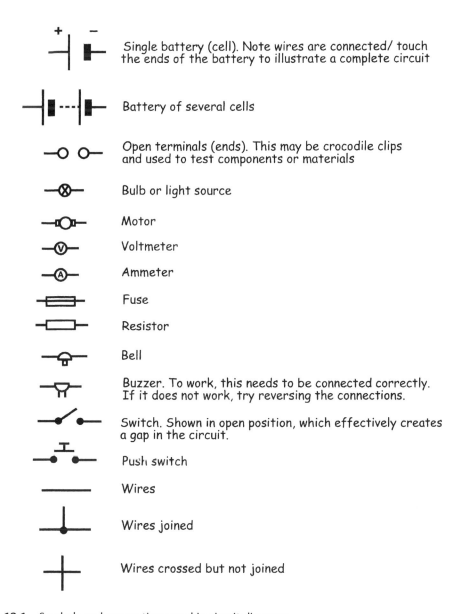

Single battery (cell). Note wires are connected/ touch the ends of the battery to illustrate a complete circuit

Battery of several cells

Open terminals (ends). This may be crocodile clips and used to test components or materials

Bulb or light source

Motor

Voltmeter

Ammeter

Fuse

Resistor

Bell

Buzzer. To work, this needs to be connected correctly. If it does not work, try reversing the connections.

Switch. Shown in open position, which effectively creates a gap in the circuit.

Push switch

Wires

Wires joined

Wires crossed but not joined

**Figure 13.1**  Symbols and conventions used in circuit diagrams

## Series circuits

There are two types of circuits, depending on how the components are arranged. A series circuit is one in which the electricity flows from one end of the battery to the other along a route that passes through each component in turn. Start with your finger on the battery in Figure 13.2 and trace the path through wires and bulbs until you get back to the battery. There is only one route that you can use, although you could go in

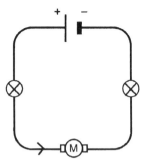

arrow shows conventional current flow

**Figure 13.2** A series circuit with two bulbs and a motor

the opposite direction! Batteries are marked to show one end as positive (+) and the other as negative (–). Although we now understand that the electrons flow from the negative end, when the conventions for drawing circuits were established this was not understood, and so the convention is to assume that electricity flows from positive to negative.

## Parallel circuits

In a parallel circuit, if you try to trace the path the electricity takes through the circuit, you come to choice points, or a branching in the circuit. This can be a simple branch, as shown in Figure 13.3, or could be more complex with several alternative routes. It is important to note that whatever path is chosen, it provides a route back to the battery. Each individual path can contain one or more components and so you can have some components arranged in series within a parallel circuit, as shown in Figure 13.4.

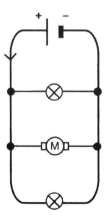

**Figure 13.3** Parallel circuit with two bulbs and a motor

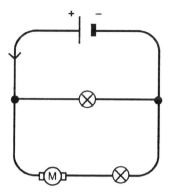

**Figure 13.4**  Parallel circuit with components in series in one branch

## Making the lamp light

There is a vast number of different devices that use electricity in order to work: computers, washing-machines, photocopiers, kettles and televisions to name a few. In order to design and build these, we need to understand how electricity flows and how components interact with each other. Earlier in this chapter, voltage, current and watts were explained.

## Resistance

One other important characteristic of circuits and their components is **resistance**. This is a measure of how easy it is for the electrons to flow. The unit of resistance is the **ohm**, abbreviated as the Greek letter omega, $\Omega$. When electrons can flow easily – for example, through copper wire – there is a low resistance. Other materials, such as the nichrome wire used in heaters, have a higher resistance. Different components have different resistances. There are some components whose purpose is to have resistance and these are called resistors. Resistors are produced with a range of values. Resistors affect the amount of current flowing and so are important devices in circuits. Sometimes a variable resistor is used. In these components the resistance can be controlled, which in turn enables the current to be altered and so affect the working of another component. Good examples of the use of variable resistors are in dimmer light switches and volume controls.

For metallic conductors, if the temperature does not change, the resistance stays the same, and so the amount of current flowing depends on the voltage. Doubling the voltage doubles the current, increasing it tenfold increases the current tenfold. Other factors affect resistance, for example the shape of the conductor. A thicker wire enables the electrons to flow more easily than in a thin one, and a longer wire has more resistance than a shorter one. Electrons naturally flow along the easiest route and so, if you connect a bulb into a circuit and then put a piece of wire in parallel, the bulb will go out because most of the current takes the easier route along the wire. You would have created a short circuit. A large current flows in the wire, which gets very hot, and the battery quickly runs down. The connecting wire does not have to be short; it is easier for the current to flow along the wire than through the bulb because its resistance is very small.

The fuse is a safety device that responds to the very large currents that would flow if there were a fault such as a short circuit in a piece of electrical equipment. Fuses are given different current ratings, three amps or 13 amps, for example. The fuse contains a piece of wire that gets hot, melts and breaks, so making a gap in the circuit and stopping the current flowing if there is a current larger than the rating. It is important to fit a fuse with the correct value; one with a higher value will enable a current that is too big to flow.

## Checking the voltage needed

When using mains electricity, the voltage is fixed, but when building simple circuits using batteries, we need to check what voltage is needed. Different components have different resistance, and some components need to have a bigger voltage so that enough current is flowing for them to work. Small light bulbs may be one and a half volts and need only one standard one-and-a-half-volt battery. But there are similar-looking bulbs which require different voltages and so may need two or three batteries in order to work. Using two standard batteries with the one-and-a-half-volt bulb will result in too much current flowing, and so the bulb will 'blow' and stop working.

This means that the voltage, provided by the battery, which is needed when setting up a circuit, depends on the components being used, how many of them there are, and whether they are arranged in series or in parallel. In a series circuit with two one-and-a-half-volt bulbs, the voltage needs to be three volts to supply enough energy to push the current through each bulb in turn. Bulbs arranged in series have a total resistance equal to their individual resistances added together. This increased resistance means that if the two bulbs need to shine as brightly as a single bulb in a circuit, you need to double the voltage by using two batteries instead of one. If two bulbs are arranged in a series circuit with one battery, then each bulb will be dimmer because less current flows through each bulb. Remember, current is measured as the rate at which the electrons are flowing, and the resistance is slowing them down. The resistance in the bulbs can be thought of as traffic jams that are controlling the traffic's speed. The important difference is that we vary our speed between traffic jams, but in a series circuit all the current flows at the same rate and this is controlled by the total resistance in the circuit.

In a parallel circuit, the voltage provided by the battery needs to be equal to the highest voltage in any one of the branch lines. In a parallel circuit using one-and-a-half volt bulbs, one standard battery will supply enough voltage for several branches, but it will run down faster. The current divides as the circuit branches and each bulb gets a share of the total current flowing. So, with two similar bulbs in a parallel circuit, each bulb has half the total current flowing through it. This is still enough to light the bulb as brightly as when there is a single bulb in a circuit because there is enough energy to push the current along the different parallel paths at the same rate. The battery has only to push the current through one 'traffic jam' or resistance. In this parallel circuit, if the bulbs have different resistances, perhaps because they are old and worn, or if components of different resistances (say, a motor and a bulb) are used, then different amounts of current flow in the different branches. This means that sometimes when we expect bulbs to be equally bright one looks dimmer than the other. The way the current divides at a branch depends on the resistance along that pathway.

These features of circuits can be summarised. If the resistance in a circuit does not change, then the current is proportional to the voltage. Resistance, current and voltage are interrelated and if values for two are measured, the third can be calculated using the relationship that voltage is equal to the current multiplied by the resistance.

## Measuring current and voltage

Current is measured using an **ammeter**. This needs to be connected in series within the circuit because it measures the rate at which electrons are flowing and so, in very simple terms, it is 'counting' electrons as they flow through the meter. A **voltmeter** is used to measure the voltage. This is measuring how much energy is available to push the current round the circuit, or how much is needed to push it through a particular component, and so this measure is taken by attaching the meter in parallel at each end of the battery or circuit component. As each component in a working circuit is also transferring energy, voltage is also a measure of how much energy is being transferred to the circuit by the battery or from the circuit by a component such as a bulb.

## Models and analogies

Electricity is invisible and so it helps us to understand what is happening in electric circuits if we have a simple way to visualise or model it. Such modelling is very useful but different models are often needed to explain different aspects, and it is important to realise where models have their limitations as representations. A very simple model of an electric circuit likens it to water flowing through pipes driven by a pump. The pump represents the battery, the pipes are the wires, and if a waterwheel or similar 'motor' is inserted into the water flow at some point, it represents a component being made to work by the electricity flowing. Stopping the pump is the same as using a switch to turn off a circuit. If the water pipe is narrowed at one point, this can represent an increased resistance, and the pump will need to pump harder for the water to flow at the same rate. The main limitation of this model is that it can lead to the incorrect belief that electricity will leak out of the wires if they become broken, but in an electric circuit a break stops the current flowing.

A useful way to model current and voltage in a circuit is to imagine people walking around the circuit, along the wires and through the components. Each person should be carrying a bucket or container. At the battery, this bucket is filled with energy and the person is pushed out along the wire. When they reach a component, such as a bulb, they pour some of the energy from the bucket into the bulb so that it lights up. They do this each time they reach a component, but they do not completely empty their bucket and they travel back to the battery to get it refilled. The bigger the current, the faster the people move and so deliver more buckets of energy.

The person walking around the circuit represents an electron and so the overall movement is the current flowing. The use of the 'bucket of energy' makes it clear that the current is not used up, but that energy is being transferred from the battery to the bulb and that it is the energy in the battery that will eventually run out. The role of the battery in supplying the voltage, both as energy to be transferred to the bulb and energy to push the electrons around the circuit, is also illustrated. By placing an obstacle, such as a small step, in the circuit, the idea of resistance as slowing the current down can be added to this model.

Series and parallel circuits can be modelled. In a parallel circuit, some of the people will deliver their bucket of energy to some components and others deliver energy to the components in a different branch. If you make a continuous line of people, they all move around at the one pace as the person at the battery is filled up and pushed on. This overcomes the incorrect idea that electrons flow at incredible speeds from the switch to the bulb every time we turn on a light.

## Electricity generation

Generation of electricity depends on the amazing interaction between electricity and magnetism. When a current flows along a wire, it produces a magnetic field and, if a wire is moved in a magnetic field, a current flows in the wire. A simple dynamo consists of a coil of wire held between the poles of a strong magnet. The coil spins and a current is produced in the wire. Spinning the wire faster, using a stronger magnet or a larger coil of wire, produces a larger current.

Powers stations are very large dynamos. Moving water, wind or steam produced by burning fossil fuels or from nuclear reactors is used to turn the dynamo. To keep producing a current, you need to change the direction of spin and this causes the current to flow in alternate directions. The result of this is that our mains electricity is AC or alternating current. All our mains electrical equipment has been designed to work using this type of current.

Direct current, which always flows in the same direction, is generated by chemical reactions that take place in batteries. As a result of the reaction, electrons are passed to the negative terminal and electrons from the circuit arriving at the positive terminal replace these. The chemicals are used up during the chemical reaction and so batteries run out and need to be replaced. Rechargeable batteries use a different chemical reaction, and passing a current from the mains through the battery can reverse the reaction. A very small current, enough to power a small clock display, is produced using the chemicals in fruits if suitable pieces of metal, such as copper and iron, are pushed into the fruit and connected to the circuit.

## Common misconceptions

Initial misconceptions about electricity are a consequence of the imprecise use of language. Electricity is often used synonymously with current. The difference between current and voltage is not appreciated and voltage and power are used interchangeably, a bigger voltage being described as more powerful. It is often thought that the current creates the voltage rather than the voltage being needed for the current to flow. It is not often recognised that the voltage exists even when no current is flowing. A one-and-a-half-volt battery has the potential to provide this voltage whether or not it is connected into a circuit.

Batteries are thought to store electricity, or current, and so run down and become flat when all this electricity or current has been used up. Batteries provide the voltage and how much voltage is indicated on the labelling, although it is more common to buy our batteries in terms of a coded size such as AA rather than by voltage. The link to energy transfer is usually missing.

Misconceptions when explaining circuits involve the electricity or current being used up and so the need for a complete circuit is not clear. Many people presented with a piece of wire, a bulb and a battery will not be able to construct a circuit in which the bulb lights. This is because they do not understand that the bulb contains wires that form part of the circuit and because they believe that the electricity or current can flow from the battery along one wire to the bulb and make it work. At the bulb this electricity or current is then used up, so there is no need to return anything to the battery. Even when the need for a complete circuit is recognised, it can be thought that the return part of the circuit does not have any current in it because the bulb has used up all the current. This return part of the circuit may be for any excess current not used up, a sort of overflow mechanism. Another idea is that the current flows from both ends of the battery to the bulb and the bulb lights because the two currents meet and interact to produce the light.

Looking at household appliances also reinforces the idea that only one wire is needed in a simple circuit. Unless it is understood that household flex contains more than one wire, and that these wires form a complete circuit, there is a natural tendency to think that current comes from the socket to the electrical equipment and gets used up. The flex is made up of the live and neutral wires, which carry current to and from the equipment, and an earth safety wire that will carry current to earth if a fault occurs.

A common misconception with bulbs connected in series is to suppose that the first bulb takes all the electricity, making it brighter and leaving none or very little for the second bulb. There follows the incorrect belief that the current in a series circuit decreases after each bulb. In fact, the current is the same at all points.

Most people recognise that batteries have a positive and negative end and that, when using them in series, batteries need to join positive to negative, but this is not related to the flow of the electrons from negative to positive. This understanding of current flow needs to be applied to the components in the circuit. For many devices, the direction the current flows does not matter but for some devices, such as buzzers and ammeters, it does.

When current is understood in terms of electrons flowing, there is a misconception that it is something like a race. All the electrons are lined up behind the switch and when it is turned on, they are free to flow. They then travel at very fast speeds in order for the lamp to light instantaneously. Understanding the atomic structure of metals and the presence of electrons helps focus on the electrons being present at *all* points *all* the time and that when a circuit is switched on, they all move round.

## Review Questions

1 Define power, voltage, current and resistance.
2 Explain why insulators can build up static electricity, but conductors do not.
3 Why is a complete circuit needed in order to get a light bulb to work? Include details of the structure of the light bulb in your explanation.
4 Explain why you should not use three one-and-a-half-volt batteries in a circuit with a single 1.5 volt bulb.
5 Explain why fewer batteries are needed to get three bulbs shining brightly if they are arranged in parallel rather than in series. Include reference to resistance, voltage and current in your explanation.

## Review Activities

1 Look at the labels on three household appliances and note the details of power and voltage given. Which are the most expensive to use?
2 Find out how to wire a three-pin plug and think about the function of each of the wires.
3 Use simple components such as batteries, a length of copper wire and small bulbs to build simple circuits. Draw diagrams of the circuits you build. Try to build the circuits drawn in Figures 13.2–13.4.
4 With some colleagues, try out the model of current and voltage given and discuss how it helps you to understand electricity and what its limitations are. What does it not help you to explain?
5 Research electricity generation, the benefits of different types of power station, such as nuclear, fossil fuel and hydro-electric, and the role of the National Grid.

# CHAPTER 14

# Energy

## QCA Units

This chapter supports the teaching of the following QCA units:

- Keeping warm

## National Curriculum

This chapter supports the following sections of the National Curriculum:

- Key stage 1 Life processes, Green plants, Changing materials, Electricity, Light and sound
- Key stage 2 Life processes, Humans and other animals: nutrition, Green plants: growth and nutrition, Reproduction, Living things in their environment: feeding relationships, Grouping and classifying materials, Electricity, Light and sound

By reading and reflecting on this chapter, you should have developed your learning about energy and be able to:

- Explain what is meant by energy.
- Identify energy transfer and conservation in a range of situations and construct energy chains.
- Describe how the energy is transferred when objects are heated or cooled.
- Consider the role of fuels as energy sources.
- Identify topics in science which can be described in terms of energy transfer.

## What is energy?

Although we refer to energy when describing people as being energetic or running out of energy, we do not often think about what this energy is. In science, energy is something that is measured in units called **joules**, abbreviated as J. Large amounts are measured in **kilojoules**, abbreviated kJ, which are equivalent to 1000 joules. The old English measure was in units called **calories**, and we commonly associate this with food values. Knowing that we can measure energy does not help us to know what it is. Unlike length or mass, we are not able to get hold of some energy and put it on our measuring device.

Energy can be transferred between things and, most importantly, the amount of energy available limits what is possible. Energy does not make things happen; having lots of energy does not make something active, but without energy nothing will happen. It can be helpful to think of energy as being like money. Having lots of money does not make you spend it, but if you have no money you cannot buy things! The amount of money that you have limits what you are able to buy; you cannot buy a new car if you only have £5. Imagine a child winding up a clockwork toy, the more the toy is wound up, the longer it will work. The child has transferred some of their own energy to the toy. The toy does not work unless it is wound up, and how long it works for depends on how much it is wound up.

Energy comes in two basic types – **potential** and **kinetic**. Potential energy is stored, or hidden, energy and so something with potential energy may not be active. A battery contains stored energy that will be transferred to a light bulb if the battery is connected into a circuit containing a bulb. Potential energy is also stored in coiled springs, stretched elastic, chemicals and in all objects that could fall if released. This height or **gravitational potential energy**, as it is called, tends to be overlooked because we expect to see objects fall and so do not think that an object raised higher also has its energy level raised, in the same way that winding a spring up more gives it more energy. The second basic type of energy is kinetic, or movement, energy. Any object that is moving has kinetic energy. The faster it moves, the more energy it has. In everyday terms, we can identify a range of different types of energy: heat, light, sound, electrical, chemical, nuclear. These are all either potential or kinetic energy.

## Energy transfer

There are two important aspects of energy that need to be appreciated. The first is that energy cannot be created or destroyed. It can be transferred, but as this happens the total amount of energy remains the same. It is not possible to lose energy. Using our money analogy, I may start with a £5 note and buy something for £3.75 and be handed my change. The total money is still £5, but it is now shared between the shopkeeper and me. Even if I drop some of the change in the street and lose it, the coins still exist; they are just no longer in my possession. The same is true of energy, and this gives it its second important characteristic – as it spreads out, it becomes less useful. The amount of energy available limits what is possible, and a large amount of energy in one place is much more useful to us.

## Energy transfer diagrams

When energy is transferred, we can show this diagrammatically as an energy transfer chain. So, when we boil a kettle of water, we transfer the energy in the electrical circuit to the water by means of the heating element in the kettle. This transfer is shown in the energy chain in Figure 14.1. As well as the desired transfer of energy from the circuit to the water, energy is also transferred in other ways as shown in Figure 14.2. All these other transfers are often incorrectly called energy losses because it is energy lost from the system that we are interested in. Energy transfers are not 100 per cent efficient in that not all of the energy goes where we want. It is a technological challenge to increase the efficiency of the machines and systems that humans have designed to transfer energy.

### Boiling water in an electric kettle

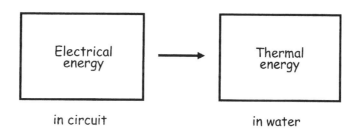

**Figure 14.1**  Energy transfer diagram

### To show energy dissipation

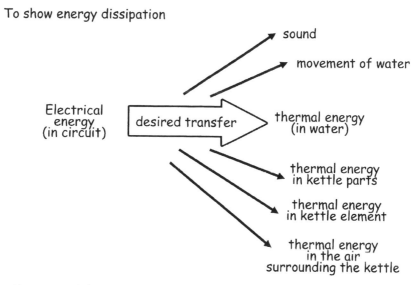

**Figure 14.2**  How energy is lost

Similar energy transfer chains can be drawn for other situations in which energy is transferred. When we lift a ball up and drop it, energy is transferred from our body to the ball as we lift it up, and this movement supplies the ball with gravitational potential energy. As the ball drops, it has kinetic energy and when it lands, we can hear sound. Also, because of friction, as the ball falls there is a warming of the air, of the ball and of the surface that it bounces off. If some energy was not transferred to the surroundings, the ball would always bounce back to its original height, because the total kinetic and potential energy of the ball would always be the same. If you listen carefully as the ball bounces, you can detect that a ball falling from a greater height makes a bigger sound. The ball higher up has more potential energy and so more to transfer as it bounces, producing a louder noise.

Think about the energy transfers involved when you use a match to light a candle, wind up a toy car, throw a paper aeroplane or drive your car. In each case, there is the desired transfer, to produce light or movement, but there are also other transfers taking place that you need to identify. Energy transfer does not need human intervention. Spontaneous energy transfer occurs when energy is transferred from a hot object to a cooler one. Eventually, all transfers result in the surroundings being warmed. This means that the available energy has been spread out between millions of molecules and is no longer in a form that humans find useful.

## Heating up and cooling down

### Temperature

Heat, or thermal energy, is kinetic energy. As explained in Chapter 7, all particles are moving about and the amount of movement depends on the temperature. **Temperature** is a measure of the average speed of the moving particles. Thermometers are calibrated or given a scale based on two fixed points so that we can measure temperature. These fixed points are the freezing and boiling points of water in standard conditions. The most common temperature scale is the **Celsius** scale in which the fixed points are zero degrees for the freezing point and 100 degrees for the boiling point. We get the two reference points by placing a fluid such as mercury or coloured alcohol inside a sealed glass container and marking the fluid levels when the container is placed, first, in melting ice and then in boiling water. These fluids expand at an even rate as the temperature increases. So, dividing the space between these points into 100 divisions produces a scale able to measure any temperature in between. The scale can also be extended using the same intervals above and below the original fixed points.

### Thermal energy and joules

Temperature is a measure of how hot or cold something is. It does not give a measure of the energy content. The kinetic energy in hot objects can be called thermal energy or heat. If you run a warm bath, with water at 30°C, it will contain very much more energy than a cup of water at the same temperature. Energy is measured in joules and in this case the number of joules of energy depends on the number of particles. Whether you have a bath or cup full of hot water, we know that it does not stay hot forever. The energy is transferred to the surroundings. All hot objects cool down when in an environment that has a lower temperature. The converse is also true. Cold objects warm up when in a warmer environment. Ice cream melts when taken out of the freezer because warm hands and warmer air then surround it. The transfer of energy is always from hot to cold and takes place spontaneously. Technology is designed either to reduce this transfer where it is considered to be a waste of energy or to make this transfer more efficient when we are interested in heating or cooling things.

## Conduction

The transfer of heat takes place in three ways: by **conduction**, **convection** and **thermal radiation**. Conduction of heat takes place quickest in solids because it depends on particles transferring some of their energy as they bump into each other. In a solid, the particles are close together and so these collisions are frequent. If one end of a metal rod is heated up, the particles at this end begin to move about faster and so bump into adjacent particles, thus causing them to move about more. This knock-on effect continues along the rod. You can model this with a group of people standing in a line. Different materials expand at different rates because the increase in movement of the particles is different in different materials.

## Convection

Convection only takes place in liquids and gases. This is because the particles are able to move about more. As individual particles gain energy and move about more rapidly, they can move away from the heat source, taking their increased energy level with them. This movement of higher energy particles forms convection currents. Warm liquids and gases rise, whilst cold ones sink. Heating water in a saucepan depends on the heat from the hotplate being conducted through the saucepan and into the water. The water particles at the bottom of the water get warmed and so move towards the surface of the water, whilst the cooler ones sink to get warmed in their turn. This means that we do not get a layer of hot water at the bottom of the pan, but all the water gradually gets hotter. If we have something in our pan that does not circulate as easily, such as a very thick sauce, we need to stir it to create a similar effect to the convection currents in water. The air circulates in a similar way and it is possible to detect the hot air rising over a hot radiator by looking carefully. To ventilate a room, it is a good idea to support this natural convection by providing fans to push the rising air back down into the room or by opening windows so that hot air leaves from the top of the window and cooler air enters lower down.

## Radiated heat

Heat or thermal radiation is a method of transferring energy that does not depend on particles. We accept that light bulbs give off light because we can see the light. In a similar way, hot objects give off thermal energy; it is just that our eyes cannot see it. We can, however, feel this warmth. Thermal cameras are designed to let us see the heat given off by various objects, and these images are colour coded so that we can recognise the hottest areas. This radiated heat can be reflected by mirrored surfaces in the same way as light can be reflected. This why electric fires often have a shiny surface behind the heating element and some people fit aluminium panels behind their household radiators. Hot objects radiate heat in all directions, and these devices work by reflecting the heat that is radiated towards the wall back into the room, to increase efficiency. Objects absorb radiated heat, and so a screen placed between yourself and a fire will absorb the heat and may leave you feeling as though you are standing in the cold.

Hotter objects radiate more heat, and matt black objects are better at giving off heat than shiny silver ones. Remember that it is an energy transfer that is involved, so it depends on the temperature difference between the object and its environment. If you place a hot matt black object somewhere cool, it will lose heat very rapidly, but if it is cold and you place it somewhere hot, it will heat up very quickly. Cold shiny silver objects stay cool when placed somewhere warm, and hot ones do not cool down as quickly as black ones when placed somewhere cold. So do we use black or silver saucepans? Do we want to heat the food quickly or keep it warm for longer? Is appearance and style more important than energy efficiency? Do we wear white or black clothes when the temperature of the surrounding air is less than body temperature, or greater than body temperature? Why are space suits and firefighting suits shiny silver? Will loose clothing increase convection currents as it flaps about?

## Insulation

Materials such as metals are very good conductors of heat, other materials transfer heat effectively by convection currents, and all objects radiate heat. If we want something to stay the same temperature, we need to insulate it. A good **thermal insulator** is one that reduces heat transfer by conduction, convection and radiation. Insulating materials work because the material itself is a poor conductor and the trapped air is unable to circulate and transfer heat by convection. In order to reduce radiated heat transfer, a shiny surface to reflect the heat back to the hot object is needed, and when we want to keep something warm, we can add a layer of aluminium foil to it. So, if you want to get your tub of ice cream home with the least amount of melting, you could wrap it in foil and layers of paper.

## Fuels as energy sources

A **fuel** is something that releases energy when it burns. More correctly, we should refer to the fuel combustion system as releasing the energy, because the oxygen involved in the chemical reaction is an important contributor to the release of energy. Lots of things burn and we detect the energy being released or transferred by the heat and light given off. Significantly, humans value materials that are concentrated sources of energy, that is, they release a lot of energy when they burn. This enables us to run machinery, keep warm and generate electricity. Such concentrated and relatively compact energy sources are called fuels. **Fossil fuels**, such as coal, oil and gas, are particularly valued. They are called fossil fuels because they are the decomposed remains of plants and animals that lived millions of years ago. When these organisms died, they did not completely decompose. Other sediments covered them and, as they became compacted, they formed layers in the rock. Fossil fuels are rich in the elements commonly found in living organisms – carbon and hydrogen – and so they are called hydrocarbons. When these burn in oxygen, they produce carbon dioxide and water and this chemical reaction releases a lot of energy.

These layers of fossil fuels were laid down in the rocks because of conditions that existed on Earth millions of years ago, and so there is a finite amount of fossil fuels available for us to mine and drill for. Our economy is very dependent on these fuels, to enable electricity to be generated and to produce petrol products for our vehicles and the chemical industry. We therefore talk about an energy crisis, but not because we can run out of energy. Energy is transferred, but not lost, and so cannot run out. What can run out are these useful fuels, and so we should refer to the fuel crisis. As fossil fuels become rarer, so their cost will inevitably rise and other ways of generating electricity for example, will become more economic. Currently, other methods that are dependent on renewable energy, such as wind, water, tides and sunlight, are being developed. Nuclear energy does not depend on fossil fuels but does use a natural resource. Although originally thought to be a long-term solution to the fuel crisis, there are significant disadvantages to this form of electricity generation, such as the radioactive waste produced and the dangers from nuclear accidents. Choices need to be made, based on an understanding of economic factors, safety, pollution and long-term projections, and these are not clear-cut issues with obvious solutions.

## Energy topics in science

### Energy transfer in organisms

In other chapters, we have thought about a variety of topics and many of these processes and changes can be explained in terms of energy transfer. Both respiration and photosynthesis are energy-transfer mechanisms. In respiration, the food that is eaten and digested reaches the body cells, where it is either used to make more of the body during growth and repair or it is the fuel for respiration. The potential energy within the food is released by a series of chemical reactions, which we call respiration, and transferred to other molecules within the cell so that all the other life processes can occur. The energy released enables movement, growth, digestion, reproduction and the detection of changes in our environment. Eventually, the energy is dissipated or spread out as it is transferred from the organism and warms the environment. Breaking down dead organisms and the process of decay is a mechanism for releasing the potential energy in the organisms. The heat released is easily detected in compost heaps.

During photosynthesis, the energy from the Sun is captured and transferred as potential energy to the sugars that are made. The Sun is the source of all the energy supporting life on Earth. The potential energy in the sugars made during photosynthesis is then transferred during the plant's metabolism to enable it to function as a living organism. The potential energy in the chemical structure of plants is the basis of food chains. Energy is transferred through food chains and so these can be represented as energy-transfer diagrams. As with other energy transfers, eating is not a very efficient process for transferring energy. Rather than all the potential energy in our food becoming potential energy within our bodies, much of it cannot be accessed. This is because there is energy in the parts of our food that we cannot digest and because the chemical processes of metabolism themselves release heat that eventually warms our surroundings. This inefficiency explains why there are fewer top carnivores than herbivores. With energy being transferred to the environment at all stages of the food chain, a very small amount of the energy taken in by the plant is transferred as far as the top of the chain. For the top carnivore to have enough energy for survival, it must rely on a great many food animals. Measuring the energy available at each level in a food chain produces diagrams called energy pyramids. These have a broad base showing the energy in the producer, and become progressively narrower at each level of consumer.

Growth can be seen as a way of storing potential energy in the chemical structure of the organism. During reproduction, the new generation is provided with an energy store to enable it to survive and grow until it is independent. Seeds have a food store in their cotyledons and eggs have food stored in the yolk. Our senses also work because of the transfer of energy. Light energy is transferred to the cells of the retina and this enables a message to be sent to the brain. With more light energy, more impulses are sent and we detect a brighter light. Detecting sound is also an energy transfer mechanism in which higher energy levels are detected as louder sounds. The eye and the ear are mechanisms that allow this transfer to take place. They are a sort of light bulb and buzzer acting in reverse!

### Energy transfer in chemical reactions

All chemical reactions transfer energy between the different atoms and molecules involved. In some reactions, the net effect is that the products of the reaction have less energy than the reactants. These reactions are called **exothermic** and they transfer the surplus energy to the environment, which heats up. Such reactions can be explosive if the rate at which this energy transfer occurs is too rapid. Other reactions have products that have more stored energy and these need energy to be provided in order for the reaction to continue. Photosynthesis is a good example of this type of reaction, which is called **endothermic**. Many reactions, even though exothermic, require an initial input of energy to get them started. When we burn materials, we need to provide an initial heating, but then the reaction continues and more heat is produced.

Fuels and food are chemicals that are very useful concentrated energy sources. Combustion and respiration are both exothermic reactions in which the potential energy is transferred. Food is an example of a fuel and some foods contain more potential or stored energy than others. Fats are particularly good energy stores and carbohydrates are good, easily accessible energy stores.

## Energy transfer during changes of state

Kinetic theory and changes of state are further examples of energy transfer. Individual particles in a material gain or lose energy and this is detected as a change of temperature, and sometimes a change of state. This energy has to come from or be given to particles and so, when an ice cream melts, the ice cream particles have energy transferred to them from particles in the air. When food is cooled in our fridges, the energy is transferred to the cooling fluid and eventually released to the air via the network of pipes at the back of the fridge. When the fridge is working, these can get very hot. Note that these are black, which makes them very good at radiating the heat as well as setting up convection currents in the surrounding air. When substances evaporate or boil, energy is transferred to the liquid particles from their surroundings to enable this to happen.

## Energy transfer in electrical circuits

We can think of electrical appliances as machines that transfer the potential energy from the electrical circuit. The current is a mechanism for carrying this potential energy round the circuit. The difference in energy levels between two points in a circuit can be measured as potential difference, also called voltage. The appliances in the circuit are mechanisms for transferring the potential energy. More potential energy, provided by a bigger voltage, enables more to be transferred. Adding an extra battery to a circuit means there is more energy available to a light bulb and so it can shine brighter, or more energy for a buzzer that then can sound louder.

## Energy and forces

It is very important to distinguish between energy and force. When energy is transferred there is often a force involved. A good example to explain the importance of making the distinction is to think about a collision between a car and a brick wall. We can think about what happens in terms of the forces involved. The force of the car when it collides with the wall is dependent on its mass and acceleration. A car speeding towards the wall pushes against the wall with a much bigger force than one moving slowly. The result of the force is to start things moving, stop them moving, or to cause a change of direction. Knowledge of forces enables us to calculate how the car and the bricks will move or stop moving.

An understanding of the energy transfers involved enables an assessment of the extent of the damage. A car moving further and faster has more kinetic energy and, therefore, much more energy is transferred to the surroundings when it stops moving as it hits the wall. The more energy that is transferred the more damage will be done or the more it will hurt. When a car collides with a wall, the distance and speed that the bricks move depends on the amount of energy transferred. The kinetic energy of the car is transferred to kinetic energy in the bricks. The energy transferred is spread out among several bricks and it takes more energy to move a large heavy brick than a small one. The bricks do not move as far or as fast as the car because some of the kinetic energy is transferred to the environment, heating it up and also giving us the sound of the impact. Some of the energy is also absorbed by the car as the structure of the car itself moves and crumples. Modern car design incorporates areas that can absorb some of the energy of collisions so that the vehicles are safer for passengers.

## Common misconceptions

Energy can be a confusing topic for many people. The obvious difficulty is that energy is invisible and often detected by something happening. This leads to the misconception that it is the energy that causes the event. Forces cause change and energy limits the extent of the change. When an event is observed, we can begin to explain what happens in terms of the forces involved or in terms of the energy transfers, and the two explanations can serve different purposes. When initially considering such events, it can simplify things if we are clear whether we want to think about the forces or the energy transfers involved.

This incorrect idea of energy making things happen leads to the idea that only things containing energy can be active, and that when the energy is used up the object will become inactive or 'dead'. This idea may develop from a very self-centred understanding of energy. Energy is needed for us to live and so is associated with self and other living things; it is something needed for life. From this incorrect viewpoint, inanimate objects do not need or have energy. We need to remember that stationary objects can have potential energy. Think about batteries or an object resting on a top shelf. In both these circumstances, the stored energy can be transferred, given the right conditions. The energy that is transferred when a circuit is made or an object falls does not magically appear as the connections are made or the shelf is removed.

Following from a personal view of energy, we learn that taking part in energetic exercise makes us tired and we talk about 'running out of energy'. In order to recover from such activity, we rest and restore our energy. This belief that our energy levels are topped up by inactivity takes no account of the need for us to tap into our energy stores of fats and carbohydrates or the role of food as a fuel. It also leads to the belief that exercise itself builds up the energy levels, a confusion between fitness and energy.

There is confusion between fuel and energy. It is incorrect to talk about food energy or fuel as a type of energy. Similarly, electricity is not energy. There are hydroelectric power stations generating electricity, but there is no hydroelectric energy, just the kinetic energy in the moving water.

Finally, if the transfer of energy is not understood, the process of keeping something warm is perceived as very different from the process of keeping something cold or insulating something, like ice cream, to stop it melting. Insulation inhibits energy transfer and there is a spontaneous transfer of energy from hot to cold areas.

Very importantly, we should never talk about energy being lost but understand that the total energy remains the same; it is transferred and gradually spreads out and becomes less useful. There is not an energy crisis but a fuel crisis, and we need to be more efficient in our energy use. Turning off lights when they are not needed stops the transfer of this very useful energy source so that it is available for transfer another time. Electricity is such a useful way of transferring energy that it is important to remember that this needs to be generated. Currently, we rely heavily on fossil fuels for this and their availability is finite.

## Review Questions

1 What are the units that energy is measured in? What are the main types of energy?

2 Explain why energy cannot be lost. What happens to it?

3 Draw an energy-transfer diagram for throwing a ball, using a hairdryer and for winding up and releasing a clockwork toy.

4 Explain why a thermos flask can keep your coffee hot and also keep your iced drink cool.

5 Explain why it hurts more when you catch a ball that is travelling fast and falling from a greater height than one that is gently thrown towards you from a metre away.

## Review Activities

1   Look at food packaging and find the details of the energy content. Do high fat and high carbohydrate food contain the most energy?

2   Drop a ball onto a hard surface from different heights. Listen to the noise of the bounce. What difference does it make when it falls a greater distance? What happens to the noise if you throw the ball down to the floor? What happens to the height of the bounce? Try to explain your observations in terms of energy transfer.

3   Build yourself a model brick wall and push toy cars into it. Watch what happens to the bricks. Change the speed of the car, what difference does it make? What do you hear?

4   Research the use of house insulation. How does it work and why does it save money?

5   Find out more about renewable energy sources. How are they used to generate electricity and what are their advantages and disadvantages?

# Glossary

| | | |
|---|---|---|
| acceleration | Ch 9 | measure of increase or decrease in speed |
| acid | Ch 8 | member of a group of chemicals that are corrosive, made from soluble non-metal oxides |
| adaptation | Ch 4 | feature that makes organisms successful competitors |
| air resistance | Ch 10 | friction force caused by movement through the air |
| alkali | Ch 8 | member of a group of chemicals that can neutralise acids, made from soluble metal oxides |
| alleles | Ch 5 | different variations of a gene |
| ammeter | Ch 13 | instrument to measure current |
| ampere/amp | Ch 13 | unit of measurement of current, rate at which electrons flow |
| amplitude | Ch 12 | measure of the extent of a to-and-fro vibration, loudness |
| anaerobic respiration | Ch 3 | respiration that does not use oxygen |
| antibiotic | Ch 2 | chemical that kills bacteria |
| artery | Ch 2 | main blood vessel carrying blood away from the heart |
| asexual | Ch 3 | reproduction with only one parent |
| atom | Ch 6 | smallest particle with the properties of the material |
| base | Ch 8 | member of a group of chemicals that can neutralise acids, made from metal oxides |
| battery | Ch 13 | more than one electrical cell, commonly a portable source of electrical energy |
| biomass | Ch 3 | the amount of organic matter in kilograms |
| biotechnology | Ch 5 | applying science and engineering to use living organisms |
| boiling | Ch 7 | change from liquid to gas at a particular temperature, $100°$ Celsius for water |
| bond | Ch 6 | linkage between atoms |

| bright | Ch 11 | reflecting or emitting a lot of light |
| brittle | Ch 6 | cracking or breaking easily |
| calorie | Ch 14 | English unit for measuring energy |
| capillary | Ch 2 | very small blood vessel in intimate contact with body tissues |
| cartilage | Ch 2 | soft, smooth, spongy tissue protecting bone ends |
| cell (electrical) | Ch 13 | source of electrical energy from chemical reaction |
| Celsius | Ch 14 | temperature scale |
| chemical change | Ch 8 | change during which new chemical materials are formed |
| chlorophyll | Ch 3 | green pigment that absorbs sunlight during photosynthesis |
| chloroplast | Ch 3 | structure that contains chlorophyll |
| chromosome | Ch 5 | structure in the cell nucleus where genes are located |
| circuit | Ch 13 | arrangement of wires and components for conducting current |
| cloning | Ch 5 | production of identical copies of cells or organisms |
| community | Ch 4 | all the living organisms in a habitat |
| compound | Ch 6 | material made of different atoms joined together |
| compressive | Ch 6 | of material, strong when pushed or squashed |
| concentrated | Ch 8 | having a high proportion of the dissolved substance present in solution |
| condensation | Ch 7 | change from gas to liquid as the material cools |
| conduction | Ch 14 | mechanism of energy transfer |
| convection | Ch 14 | mechanism of heat transfer, giving rise to moving liquid or gas |
| current | Ch 13 | flow of electrons |
| cytoplasm | Ch 5 | area in cells where metabolism takes place |
| decibel | Ch 12 | measure of the loudness of sounds |
| density | Ch 6 & 9 | a material's mass divided by its volume |
| diffusion | Ch 7 | gradual spreading out of particles |
| distillation | Ch 7 | process of boiling and cooling liquids used to separate liquids from mixtures |
| DNA | Ch 5 | genetic material of the chromosomes |
| dominant | Ch 5 | feature of some alleles that means they are expressed |
| ductile | Ch 6 | of material, able to be shaped and moulded |
| dull | Ch 11 | absorbing light and reflecting a little |
| echo | Ch 12 | reflected sound |
| eclipse | Ch 11 | shadow formed when the Sun, Earth and Moon are aligned |
| ecology | Ch 4 | the scientific study of the environment |
| ecosystem | Ch 4 | defined area studied by ecologists |

| | | |
|---|---|---|
| egestion | Ch 3 | removal of undigested food from the end of the digestive system |
| elastic | Ch 2 & 6 | able to stretch when pulled and return to original size |
| electrical conductor | Ch 13 | material that allows electrons to flow through it |
| electrical insulator | Ch 13 | material that resists the flow of electrons, and which can build up a static charge |
| electron | Ch 6 | sub-atomic particle in shells or orbits, having a negative charge |
| element | Ch 6 | basic building block of materials |
| endothermic | Ch 14 | chemical reaction that requires energy to be provided for it to continue |
| environment | Ch 4 | general term for everything around us |
| evaporation | Ch 7 | change from liquid to gas that takes place at all temperatures |
| evolution | Ch 3, 4 & 5 | changes to living organisms over time |
| excretion | Ch 3 | removal of waste products that result from metabolism |
| exothermic | Ch 14 | chemical reaction that releases energy as it continues |
| expansion | Ch 7 | increase in size that occurs as a material is heated |
| flammable | Ch 8 | of material, tending to burn when heated |
| food chain | Ch 4 | diagram showing simple feeding relationships |
| food web | Ch 4 | diagram showing complex interrelated feeding relationships |
| fossil fuel | Ch 14 | coal, oil and gas; fuels made from organisms that died millions of years ago |
| free fall | Ch 10 | a downward acceleration resulting from gravitational force |
| frequency | Ch 12 | number of to-and-fro movements in a vibration |
| friction | Ch 9 | force that slows down objects or provides grip |
| fuel | Ch 8 & 14 | material that combines with oxygen when it burns and releases energy |
| gene | Ch 5 | coded information unit on the chromosome |
| germination | Ch 3 | initial sprouting of a seed |
| gravitational potential energy | Ch 14 | energy that results from height |
| gravity | Ch 3 & 9 | force that pulls things down towards the centre of the Earth |
| growth | Ch 3 | making new organic material to increase the number of cells or replace cells |
| habitat | Ch 4 | defined area where organisms live |
| hard | Ch 6 | of material, difficult to scratch or dent |

| hertz | Ch 12 | unit of measurement of frequency |
|---|---|---|
| heterotrophic | Ch 5 | feeding by eating other organisms |
| igneous rock | Ch 8 | rock resulting from volcanic activity |
| image | Ch 11 | picture formed in a mirror |
| immunisation | Ch 2 | injecting dead or inactive microbes to stimulate defence against disease |
| inertia | Ch 9 | resistance of an object to acceleration or deceleration |
| insoluble | Ch 6 | of substances, unable to dissolve in water |
| joint | Ch 2 | where two bones meet; can be fixed or movable |
| joule | Ch 2 & 14 | unit of measurement of energy |
| kilojoule | Ch 2 & 14 | one thousand joules |
| kilowatt-hour | Ch 13 | measurement of the rate at which electricity is used |
| kinetic energy | Ch 14 | movement energy |
| life cycle | Ch 3 | development stages in the life of an organism |
| ligament | Ch 2 | strong, flexible, slightly elastic material holding bones together in a joint |
| loudness | Ch 12 | volume of sound dependent on size of the vibration causing it |
| lustrous | Ch 6 | shiny |
| magma | Ch 8 | molten rock below the Earth's crust |
| magnetic field | Ch 10 | area of magnetic force surrounding a magnet |
| mass | Ch 9 | amount of matter measured in kilograms |
| matt | Ch 11 | having a rough surface that does not reflect light well |
| meiosis | Ch 5 | cell division that halves the number of chromosomes, produces gametes |
| melting | Ch 7 | change from solid to liquid state as a material is heated |
| metabolism | Ch 2 & 5 | the chemical activity in cells |
| metamorphic rock | Ch 8 | rock that results from further heating of and pressure on sedimentary rocks |
| micro-organism/ microbe | Ch 2 | microscopic organism; bacteria, viruses, fungi |
| mitosis | Ch 5 | cell division that maintains the chromosome number, the basis of growth |
| mixture | Ch 6 | combination of elements or compounds in which the constituents are not chemically bonded together |
| molecule | Ch 6 | two or more atoms bonded together |
| momentum | Ch 9 | force needed to stop a moving object |
| movement | Ch 3 | life process by which an organism, or parts of it, changes its location |
| natural selection | Ch 3 & 5 | process by which environmental factors control populations |

| neutral | Ch 8 | neither acidic nor alkaline |
|---|---|---|
| neutron | Ch 6 | sub-atomic particle in nucleus with no charge |
| Newton | Ch 9 & 10 | unit in which forces are measured |
| nucleus (cell biology) | Ch 5 | area in cells containing chromosomes |
| nucleus | Ch 6 | central part of an atom, containing sub-atomic particles |
| nutrient | Ch 2 | chemical needed as food |
| nutrition | Ch 3 | feeding by eating and digesting or by photosynthesis |
| ohm | Ch 13 | unit of measurement of electrical resistance |
| opaque | Ch 6 & 11 | of material, not allowing light to pass through |
| orbit | Ch 11 | path followed by planets and moons |
| oxide | Ch 8 | chemical formed when substances combine with oxygen |
| penumbra | Ch 11 | area of partial shadow |
| pH | Ch 8 | scale that measures acidity or alkalinity |
| photosynthesis | Ch 3 | process by which plants make their own food |
| pitch | Ch 12 | frequency of a note, whether high or low |
| plaque | Ch 2 | layer of food, bacteria and acid, which develops on teeth after eating |
| plasma | Ch 2 | liquid part of the blood, containing dissolved substances |
| plastic | Ch 6 | of material, becoming permanently stretched when pulled |
| pole | Ch 10 | end of a magnet, having a strong magnetic field |
| pollination | Ch 3 | transfer of pollen from anther to stigma |
| potential energy | Ch 14 | stored or hidden energy |
| power | Ch 13 | rate at which electricity is used, measured in watts |
| primary consumer | Ch 4 | herbivore, an organism that feeds on plants |
| producer | Ch 4 | green plant, which makes its own food |
| proton | Ch 6 | sub-atomic particle in the nucleus, positively charged |
| pulse | Ch 2 | rhythmic contraction in arteries, detected at pulse points |
| recessive | Ch 5 | feature of some alleles which means they are not expressed by the organism, but can be passed to the next generation |
| reflection | Ch 11 | image seen in a mirror surface |
| resistance | Ch 13 | material property that impedes the flow of electrons |
| resonance | Ch 12 | phenomenon in which objects vibrate at the same frequency as the original vibration |
| respiration | Ch 2 & 3 | chemical breakdown of sugars to release energy, which takes place in cells |
| rigid | Ch 6 | of material, stiff and inflexible |

| | | |
|---|---|---|
| secondary consumer | Ch 4 | animal that feeds on a herbivore |
| sedimentary rock | Ch 8 | rock formed from layers of transported weathered volcanic rock or from dead organisms which settle on the seabed |
| sensitivity | Ch 3 | ability to detect changes in our internal and external environments |
| shadow | Ch 11 | area where light does not reach because it is being blocked by an object |
| shiny | Ch 6 & 11 | smooth and reflecting a lot of light |
| solidifying | Ch 7 | change from liquid to solid as a material cools |
| soluble | Ch 6 | of substances, able to dissolve in water |
| solute | Ch 7 | a solid material that dissolves |
| solvent | Ch 7 | liquid, often water, in which a solid dissolves |
| sonar | Ch 12 | use of echoes to detect distances and differences in surfaces |
| sonorous | Ch 6 | making a ringing sound when struck |
| speed | Ch 9 | a measure of how fast something is travelling |
| strong | Ch 6 | of material, difficult to break |
| strong (acid) | Ch 8 | with very acidic properties |
| synovial fluid | Ch 2 | lubricant fluid between bones in moveable joints |
| temperature | Ch 14 | measurement of how hot something is |
| tendon | Ch 2 | non-elastic structure that attaches muscles to bones |
| tensile | Ch 6 | of material, strong when pulled |
| terminal velocity | Ch 10 | speed reached by a falling object when gravity and air resistance are balanced |
| thermal insulator | Ch 14 | material that reduces heat transfer |
| thermal radiation | Ch 14 | heat transfer without particles |
| timbre | Ch 12 | sound quality, depends on source or instrument |
| tissue fluid | Ch 2 | fluid derived from blood that surrounds cells |
| tough | Ch 6 | of material, not easy to break |
| translucent | Ch 11 | of material, allowing light through but which cannot be seen through |
| transparent | Ch 6 & 11 | of material, allowing light to pass through and to be seen through |
| transpiration | Ch 3 | water loss by evaporation from plant shoots and leaves |
| umbra | Ch 11 | area of deepest shadow |
| Universal Indicator | Ch 8 | substance that shows different colours at different pH |
| variation | Ch 3 & 5 | difference |
| vein | Ch 2 | blood vessel containing blood that is returning to the heart |

| velocity | Ch 9 | a measure of how fast, and in which direction, something is travelling |
| vibration | Ch 12 | rapid to-and-fro motion |
| volt | Ch 13 | unit of measurement of voltage |
| voltage | Ch 13 | measure of energy available to push the current |
| voltmeter | Ch 13 | instrument to measure voltage |
| watt | Ch 13 | unit that measures power |
| wavelength | Ch 12 | measure of distance between individual vibration movements |
| weight | Ch 10 | measured in Newtons, property of an object resulting from the pull of gravity |

# Bibliography

Asoko, H. and De Boo, M. (2001) *Analogies and Illustrations – representing ideas in primary science.* Hatfield: ASE.

Atkinson, S. and Fleer, M. (eds) (1995) *Science with Reason*, London: Hodder & Stoughton Educational.

Browne, N. (ed.) (1991) *Science and Technology in the Early Years*, Buckingham: Open University Press.

Carlton, K. and Parkinson, E. (1994) *Physical Sciences: A Primary Teachers Guide*, London: Cassell.

Chaille, C. and Britain, L. (1991) *The Young Child as Scientist*, New York: HarperCollins.

CLIS (1987) *Children's Learning in Science Project, Information leaflet*, Centre for Studies in Science and Mathematics Education, University of Leeds.

De Boo, M. (2000) *Science 3–6 Laying the Foundations in the Early Years*, Hatfield: ASE.

DfEE and QCA (1999) *Science: The National Curriculum for England*, London: HMSO.

Driver, R. (1988) 'A constructivist approach to curriculum development', in Fensham, P. *Developments and Dilemma in Science Education*, Lewes: Falmer Press.

Driver, R., Guesne, E. and Tiberghien, A. (eds) (1985) *Children's Ideas in Science*, Buckingham: Open University Press.

Driver, R., Squires, A., Rushworth, P. and Wood-Robinson, V. (1997) *Making Sense of Secondary Science.* London: Routledge.

Farrow, S. (1996) *The Really Useful Science Book*, London: Falmer Press.

Feasey, R. (1999) *Primary Science and Literacy Links*, Hatfield: ASE.

Feasey, R. and Gallear, B. (2000) *Primary Science and Numeracy Links*, Hatfield: ASE.

Feasey, R. and Gallear, B. (2001) *Primary Science and ICT*, Hatfield: ASE.

Gipps, C. and Stobart, G. (1993) *Assessment: a Teachers' Guide to the Issues*, London: Hodder & Stoughton.

Harlen, W. (ed.) (1985) *Taking the Plunge*, Oxford: Heinemann Educational.

Harlen, W. (2000) *Teaching, Learning and Assessing Science 5–12*, London: Paul Chapman.

Harlen, W. (2004) *The Teaching of Science in Primary Schools*, London: David Fulton.

Hollins, M. and Whitby, V. (eds) (2001) *Progression in Primary Science* (2nd edition), London: David Fulton.

Johnsey, R., Peacock, G., Sharp, J. and Wright, D. (2002) *Primary Science: Knowledge and Understanding (Achieving QTS)*, Exeter: Learning Matters.

Kennedy, J. (ed.) (1997) *Primary Science Knowledge and Understanding*, London: Routledge.

Meadows, J. (2004) *Science and ICT in Primary Schools*, London: David Fulton.

Monk, M. and Osborne, J. (2000) *Good Practice in Science Teaching: what research has to say*, Buckingham: Open University.

Naylor, S. and Keogh, B. (1996) *Concept Cartoons in Science Education*, Sandbach: Millgate House.

Nuffield Primary Science, *Science Processes and Concept Exploration* (1995) *Living Things in their Environment, Teachers' Guide, Ages 5–7*, London: Collins Educational. Other titles in the series include *Living Processes, Variety of Life, Materials, Using Energy, Forces and Movement, Earth and Space, Rocks, Soils and Weather, Light, Electricity and Magnetism*.

Nuffield Primary Science, *Science Processes and Concept Exploration* (1995) *Living Things in their Environment, Teachers' Guide, Ages 7–12*, London: Collins Educational. Other titles in the series include *Living Processes, Variety of Life, Materials, Using Energy, Forces and Movement, Earth and Space, Rocks, Soils and Weather, Light, Electricity and Magnetism*.

Osborne, J., Black, P., Smith, M. and Meadows, J. (1990) *Primary SPACE Research Reports, Light*, Liverpool: University of Liverpool Press.

Osborne, J., Black, P., Smith, M. and Meadows, J. (1991) *Primary SPACE Research Reports, Electricity*, Liverpool: University of Liverpool Press.

Osborne, J., Wadsworth, P., Black, P. and Meadows, J. (1994) *Primary SPACE Research Reports, The Earth in Space*, Liverpool: University of Liverpool Press.

Osborne, J., Wadsworth, P. and Black, P. (1992) *Primary SPACE Research Reports, Processes of Life*, Liverpool: University of Liverpool Press.

Peacock, G. (1998) *QTS Science for Primary Teachers: An audit and self study guide*, London: Letts.

QCA/DfEE (1998) *Science: A scheme of work for Key Stages 1 and 2*, London: QCA.

QCA/DfEE (1998) *Science Teacher's Guide*, London: QCA.

QCA/DfEE (2000) *Science Teacher's Guide Update*, London: QCA.

Qualter, A. (1996) *Differentiated Primary Science*, Buckingham: Open University Press.

Russell, T. and Watt, D. (1990) *Primary SPACE Research Reports, Evaporation and Condensation*, Liverpool: University of Liverpool Press.

Russell, T. and Watt, D. (1990) *Primary SPACE Research Reports, Growth*, Liverpool: University of Liverpool Press.

Russell, T., Longden, K. and McGuigan, L. (1991) *Primary SPACE Research Reports, Materials*, Liverpool: University of Liverpool Press.

Russell, T., Bell, D., Longden, K. and McGuigan, L. (1993) *Primary SPACE Research Reports, Rocks, Soil and Weather,* Liverpool: University of Liverpool Press.

Russell, T., McGuigan, L. and Hughes, A. (1998) *Primary SPACE Research Reports, Forces,* Liverpool: University of Liverpool Press.

Sherrington, R. (ed.) (1998) *ASE Guide to Primary Science Education,* Cheltenham: Stanley Thornes (Publishers) Ltd.

Watt, D. and Russell, T. (1990) *Primary SPACE Research Reports, Sound,* Liverpool: University of Liverpool Press.

Wenham, M. (1995) *Understanding Primary Science Ideas, Concepts and Explanations,* London: Paul Chapman.

Wenham, M. (2001) *200 Science Investigations for Young Students,* London: Paul Chapman.

# Index

An environmentally friendly book printed and bound in England by www.printondemand-worldwide.com

PEFC Certified

This product is
from sustainably
managed forests
and controlled
sources

www.pefc.org

PEFC/16-33-415

This book is made entirely of chain-of-custody materials; FSC materials for the cover and PEFC materials for the text pages.

#0406 - 300113 - C0 - 246/189/11 - PB